Growing up with Harry

Sherman Baldwin

Also by Sherman Baldwin

Ironclaw: A Navy Carrier Pilot's War Experience

Growing up with Harry

Stories of Character

Sherman Baldwin

Author of *Ironclaw*

iUniverse, Inc.
New York Bloomington Shanghai

Growing up with Harry
Stories of Character

iUniverse books may be ordered through booksellers or by contacting:

iUniverse
1663 Liberty Drive
Bloomington, IN 47403
www.iuniverse.com
1-800-Authors (1-800-288-4677)

Because of the dynamic nature of the Internet, any Web addresses
or links contained in this book may have changed
since publication and may no longer be valid.

The views expressed in this work are solely those of the author and do not
necessarily reflect the views of the publisher, and the publisher hereby
disclaims any responsibility for them.

ISBN: 978-0-595-45291-0 (pbk)
ISBN: 978-0-595-69807-3 (cloth)
ISBN: 978-0-595-89605-9 (ebk)

Printed in the United States of America

For Harry's grandchildren:

Henry, Lucy, Shane, Tommy, and Allison

Contents

Acknowledgments

I want to thank the following family members and dear friends who have taken the time to read drafts and help me shape this book. I owe a heartfelt thanks to Andrew Auchincloss, Alex Baldwin, Martha Baldwin, Keith Berwick, Scott Bush, Don Lamm, Eric Motley, Jacob Ner David, Maria Sette, David Segel, Lindley Shutz, Sue Siegal and Lynn Utter.

I wrote this book, as I did my first book, in my rare spare time over many late nights and weekends while working full time in a demanding job. So most of all, I want to thank Alice, my wife. In my first book, I wrote that she is my strongest supporter, my most honest critic, my best friend, and my greatest love. After fifteen years of marriage, these words still describe my feelings for Alice. I am a lucky man; and Alice is a beautiful, elegant, intelligent and above all else, an extremely patient woman.

Preface

My original purpose for *Growing up with Harry* was to share memories of my dad, Harry, with my children. My grandfather and namesake died before I got to know him, and I always wondered what I'd missed. What stories did I never get the chance to hear and learn from? I wanted to give my children and grandchildren stories about my dad so that they wouldn't need to ask that same question.

Then I had a conversation with Walt Shill, a colleague of mine, which inspired a larger purpose for the book. During a car ride we shared to the Atlanta airport, which should have lasted thirty minutes, but due to horrible traffic, was transformed into a two-hour ordeal, we swapped stories, both hilarious and serious, about our fathers. We laughed together, we remembered, and we grew thankful for the lessons we had learned from our experiences.

During this conversation, it became clear to me that every family has stories—moments when character is revealed and values are shaped— and that all families can benefit from telling and reliving those stories, because doing so reinforces universal lessons and values that come from our shared experiences. Families are a sum of their stories. Whether the stories are happy or sad, they have value because they pass life lessons on to the next generations.

Stories that teach moral character are particularly valuable. Character is something that is tested in each of us every day, and the seeds of character, or lack thereof, are planted in a family by our daily actions. Let me give you an example.

One day last fall, I went to see a school music assembly that my daughter, Lucy, was in. Since I was a bit late, the parking lot was already lined with cars, so I resigned myself to the reality of parking across the street and hiking a long way back to the school. Parking far away was my penalty for being late. As I was turning to leave the parking lot, a silver

Porsche convertible pulled in front of me. The car slowed to a stop. The driver jumped out, walked over to the small, portable No Parking—Fire Exit sign that was placed by the auditorium's back door, picked it up, and moved it onto the grass. He then parked in the space where the sign had been. Shaking my head, I drove across the street to park and walked back to the school. I could only wonder what lessons of character this man's children were learning from him.

Given the turbulent times in which we live today, with the pace of change only accelerating, I believe that, more than ever before, it is important to ground this generation of children with stories of character. That said, this collection of stories is not aimed at only parents and grandparents. Children can benefit from reading this book, and then asking their parents and grandparents to tell them their families' stories. I know that every family is different—my family may hold values that are different from yours, for example—but I hold that some values are universal and need to be reinforced in all children. *Growing up with Harry* is an attempt to capture some of these universal values. My hope is that this book will inspire you to recall and share your own experiences—those that represent the fabric and moral character of your family—both with your own family and with the world around you.

***

When I was a boy of fourteen, my father was so ignorant I could hardly stand to have the old man around. But when I got to be twenty-one, I was astonished at how much he had learned in seven years.
—Mark Twain

Introduction

All families have moments that they will never forget. One such moment for our family happened in the living room of my parents' house in Roxbury, Connecticut, in January of 1997, when Harry said to my wife, Alice, and me, "Sit down. I have something important to tell you."

"What's up, Dad?" I asked, as I moved to sit next to him. As I sat down, I glanced at my mother, who was on the adjacent sofa, looking down at her shoes. She clearly could not bear to look at me. Alice sat down on the sofa on the other side of the coffee table from me. I was seated in a chair next to Harry, who was in his usual spot: what everyone in the family knew as "Harry's chair."

For my entire life, I had looked at my father and seen a strong, vibrant, and intelligent man. At that moment, I saw in him a frailty that I had rarely, if ever, seen before. And then he spoke.

"I have Lou Gehrig's disease, and there is no known cure." As he uttered these words, a wave of emotion struck him, and he visibly shuddered. His eyes welled with tears, and he looked at the ground. I knelt beside his chair and hugged him; Alice held his hand. Time stood still for a few minutes as we all thought about the past and the future. Nine months later, Harry died.

It has now been ten years since Harry died, and not a day goes by that I don't wish I could speak with him to ask his advice, to tell him a joke, to listen to a story, or just to talk about the game the night before. Over the past decade, I have had many moments when I wondered, "What would Harry do?" This collection of stories attempts to answer this question by capturing the heart and mind of a man of true character.

Harry was a product of the World War II era, part of what has been called America's "greatest generation." As such, he grew up in a time when people were not shy about speaking of honor, duty, courage, commitment, honesty, integrity, persistence, and love of family. Harry understood that the foundation of character and success in life are rooted in these characteristics.

Harry's actions were important to him, not because of what they would make someone else think of him, but because of what his actions made him think of himself. His actions taught me that character is about what you do when nobody is looking. Harry also taught me to try to do the right thing when faced with a difficult choice, to be a good friend, and to persevere when life seems hard. In turn, happiness and fulfillment come from being a part of something larger than yourself.

I want to share some stories of character and a grounded set of values that I learned from growing up with a man I called Dad, but who, to most everyone else, was known as Harry. He was not perfect, but I was lucky to have him as my father.

While he was not a reader of poetry, Harry would have loved this poem:

To Be of Use

The people I love the best
jump into work head first
without dallying in the shallows
and swim off with sure strokes almost out of sight.
They seem to become natives of that element,
the black sleek heads of seals
bouncing like half submerged balls.

I love people who harness themselves, an ox to a heavy cart,
who pull like water buffalo, with massive patience,
who strain in the mud and the muck to move things forward,
who do what has to be done, again and again.

I want to be with people who submerge
in the task, who go into the fields to harvest
and work in a row and pass the bags along,

who stand in the line and haul in their places,
who are not parlor generals and field deserters
but move in a common rhythm
when the food must come in or the fire be put out.

The work of the world is common as mud.
Botched, it smears the hands, crumbles to dust.
But the thing worth doing well done
has a shape that satisfies, clean and evident.
Greek amphoras for wine or oil,
Hopi vases that held corn, are put in museums
but you know they were made to be used.
The pitcher cries for water to carry
and a person for work that is real.

From *Circles on the Water*, by Marge Piercy
Copyright 1982, Marge Piercy
Reprinted by permission of Alfred A. Knopf, Inc.

Harry

Harry stood six feet tall, and one of his friends from college once described him to me as "the strongest man I have ever known." For years while growing up, I thought this was a compliment about his physical strength, which was quite impressive. He broke many crowbars prying rocks out of our property in Roxbury, Connecticut. But as I grew older, I came to understand that his friend was paying him a deeper compliment—about the strength of his character.

Harry was a simple man. This is not to say that he was not intelligent, because he was. What I mean to say is that Harry never made things too complicated. In his view, you should work hard, play hard, love your family, and be truly committed to your friends and to your community.

His close-cropped dark hair turned gray over the years, and his nose was slightly crooked from playing football. His eyes were a sparkly blue. His left knee was scarred from surgery to correct athletic injuries, and his slightly pudgy tummy made him seem like an affectionate Buddha, which was a term of endearment my mom often used for Harry. In fact, on his bureau in his bedroom was a five-inch wooden sculpture of a laughing Buddha, which was a gift from Mom early in their marriage.

I loved the top of Harry's bureau. Today it is my bureau, and though I have grown accustomed to my things being on top of it, I still remember his stuff. There was a beautiful photograph of Mom in her wedding dress. There was a picture of my grandparents. In the center was a small wicker basket where Harry emptied his pockets of change every evening. Next to the wicker basket was the little dark brown Buddha carved out of mahogany.

1

The big smile and the round, soft belly of the carved Buddha gave off a true aura of contentment that enveloped his bureau. For Harry, everything had its place, and his bureau was a reflection of this. He was a vibrant, healthy, and athletic man throughout his entire life, until a terrible disease took him from all of us far too soon.

Above all, Harry was a man of character. He taught me that character is always doing the right thing, even when nobody is looking. Character is about having a strong moral compass that helps you do the right thing when faced with difficult choices.

Symbols

Roxbury, Connecticut, is a quiet place. Our house in Roxbury is a modest colonial saltbox that sits alongside a dirt road behind five tall sturdy maple trees and an old stone wall. The house is surrounded by two acres of mowable lawn, along with fourteen acres of hay fields and woods. The land is fairly flat, but it does calmly undulate along the base of Good Hill. A tiny stream runs across the property and several other stone walls divide up the fields. This piece of land in the rolling hills of western Connecticut holds many memories for my family, but above all else, it was Harry's place.

There are two enduring symbols at our home in Roxbury. One is the old locomotive bell on the stone wall behind the house, and the other is the wellstone stuck in the ground by the post and rail fence in the big field. The wellstone acted as the foundation for the well house. It is a large, flat stone slab measuring five feet long by three feet wide by five inches thick. For years, a bucket and the rope attached to it passed through the twenty-four-inch circular hole in its center to collect the water from the well. Harry installed both of these enduring symbols, the bell and the wellstone, on the property in Roxbury.

The old locomotive bell was brought to Roxbury when my grandparents decided to sell their home in Redding, Connecticut. The bell had been on the locomotive of a train that ran from Boston to Maine. It is cast iron and must weigh at least five hundred pounds. Not only is it heavy, but since it has moving parts, it is quite awkward and difficult to carry. The day the bell showed up in Roxbury was quite a memorable event.

Harry and his friend Whitey McNamara were determined to move the bell onto the stone wall behind our house. This planned perch was over one hundred yards from where Whitey parked his pickup truck. The weight of the bell forced Whitey's truck to squat over the rear wheels and pitch up in the front. Whitey was generally a cheerful man who was accustomed to hard work since he was the owner of the nursery in Redding, where the bell had previously rested on my grandparents' property. That said, the task at hand—and the impact of the bell on his truck—made him frown. There was only a small gap in the stone wall, too small for the truck to pass through and so they needed to improvise. They drew on ancient history to solve the problem. The two men were like the ancient Egyptians as they rolled the bell through gap in the stone wall and across the grass fields on a series of logs. Like building the pyramids, it was a slow and laborious process.

After several hours of sweat and toil, Harry and Whitey finally positioned the bell on the stone wall. For years, the bell symbolized "Soup's on." My brother, Alex, and I would go exploring in the woods all morning. We would build forts and dam up the stream, and the only thing that would bring us back to the house was Mom ringing the bell. I still think of a hot dinner whenever I hear the sound of a bell.

The other curious symbol on the property is the wellstone, which, again, was the foundation for the little well house that was located directly behind the house. The stone must have weighed several hundred pounds. The pulley system that held the bucket was suspended from the roof of the well house, and the bucket traveled up and down for years, gathering water through the hole in the wellstone.

When my parents decided to expand our house, they made the decision to remove the well and the wellstone. It wasn't until we tore down the well house that we realized that this wellstone had quite an intriguing shape. Harry felt that this special stone should remain on the property since it had been there for many more years than our family had. With that thought, we decided to make it the centerpiece of a small garden on the gently sloping lawn behind the house.

Because the stone was so heavy, we used the same Egyptian approach that we had used to move the train bell. We rolled it on a series of logs, moving it up and across the sloping lawn. I clearly remember digging the hole with Harry for the wellstone. We dreaded digging any hole in the land, whether for planting a shrub or for something more unusual, like erecting the wellstone.

We had two shovels and one crowbar to make the hole into which we would place our creation. The digging was easy at first. The first few inches of soil were deceptively soft. The shovel blades cut into the earth under our feet in a satisfying way. Those first few shovelfuls of grass and topsoil made each of us smile. Just as we started to break a sweat and think, "This isn't so bad," we heard the *clink* of metal on rock, and we knew this was just the beginning of a long struggle.

After a while, my young body needed a rest, but I will never forget watching as Harry continued to wrestle with the submerged rock. He circled around it and checked every angle. He tried to assess where the edges were so that he could size up the problem. Eventually, it became pitched combat: a focused battle between man and rock. Harry's primary weapons were his five-foot-long crowbar and his shovel. He would dig around the edges and then jam the crowbar in a well-placed spot around the rock. He would pry the rock up, trying to displace it from the clutches of the earth. Harry kept repeating this process of *jam, pry, pry, pry; jam, pry, pry, pry* until the rock finally budged. Even the slightest movement gave Harry hope. He knew he would win the battle; he always did. He just didn't know how long it would take.

Harry continued to pry more fervently in hopes of changing the situation. The crowbar was bent under Harry's weight, and finally there was a loud *crack* that sounded vaguely like a shot from a gun. He had broken the crowbar with his bare hands. Harry tumbled to the ground, holding only two feet of the five-foot crowbar in his hands. Getting up and dusting himself off, Harry proclaimed with a satisfied smile, "It looks like this is going to be a two-crowbar rock."

After a trip to the supply company, Harry used his new crowbar to loosen the earth's grip on the large stone. Eventually, we won the battle, and the rock was extricated from the hole. Then we continued to shovel and pull out smaller rocks for the next hour, until we finally created a hole befitting the monument we were erecting.

We enjoyed pushing our artistic and creative talents. As we positioned the rock in the ground, we thought of it as our piece of abstract art. To this day, the wellstone stands straight up from that hole, three feet above the ground. Over the years, many little faces have protruded from the hole in its center, asking to have their pictures taken. It is one of my favorite spots on the Roxbury property because it was such a family endeavor. Each of us played a role, whether it was rolling the wellstone up the hill on logs, digging the hole, or planting the flowers in the garden surrounding it. When it was done, it was a family place.

We always laughed and thought of it as our "act of God" garden. It was as if God had thrown the rock down at us, and it had stuck in the ground just so. We, as mere mortals, had planted a garden to honor the "stone" from above. Now, as I reflect on this special stone more than ever, I still view it as an act of God because of the way our family created such a long-lasting cherished memory from the act of sticking a stone in the ground. I believe that Harry had a deep understanding of how timeless certain things could be.

The bell and the wellstone are still there today, and whenever I go to Roxbury, I touch them and reflect on the special vision Harry had: to build things that would last. I also remember his battle with the rock, as well as the persistence he demonstrated to me that day. While the struggle was hard, I never had any doubt about the outcome. These are symbols of our family—of its steadfastness, its persistence, and its timelessness.

***

Symbols are the imaginative signposts of life.
—Margot Asquith

Our home in Roxbury, Connecticut (circa. 1970)

Work

During the week, Harry was a lawyer, and he would advise his clients on how best to take care of their families. He was well respected as a lawyer because he cared deeply about his clients. His father and his grandfather had done the same work, and he was a member of the same law firm: Lord, Day & Lord. I remember his working nights in our living room, with a yellow legal pad of paper and plenty of pencils.

The law exercised his mind during the week, but in Roxbury, he loved to exercise his body by working outside. Our home in Roxbury is nestled on a ridgeline along a dirt road, and it overlooks a densely wooded valley. The dirt road penetrates the forest, with limbs from the trees providing a protective canopy. In front, five old sprawling maple trees grow on one side of the road, and on the other side lies the foundation of a sunken barn. The house itself is quite old, and Harry loved the way that the creaky floorboards speak to you as you walk through it. There are no true right angles in the house, as its foundation has settled over time.

Harry loved Roxbury, and he loved the weekends, because that's when he was in his element. He worked hard during the week, but he really tried to relax on the weekends. The funny thing is that the way he relaxed was by doing more work. It was a different kind of work than what he did during the week. It brought sweat to his brow, and it made him happy.

In the fall, he raked leaves and chopped wood. In the winter, he cleared brush and had brush fires. In the spring, he cleaned up the gardens and prepared for summer. In the summer, it was gardening and mowing. Every now and again, a big project or special idea would become Harry's focus for the better part of a weekend, if not a month.

No matter what the work, Harry rarely wore gloves. When planting shrubs or flowers, I remember watching him smile with a sense of contentment as he plunged his hands deep into the soil. He would sweat profusely, and at the end of the day, he enjoyed a beer. He would smile a knowing smile that said he was pleased with what he had accomplished that day.

When I was young, I didn't think this was a very fun way to spend the weekends, but as I grew older, I began to help him more often. I began to understand the pride that he took in his work. Together, my parents made a beautiful home in Roxbury.

One fall day, Harry was chopping firewood, and my brother and I were playing outside. Harry asked us if we would like to help stack the wood. Alex said, "No thanks, Dad. We're playing. Why don't you come play with us?"

"No thanks, Alex," said Harry. He kept working, and we kept playing. At the time, Alex was learning to read, and we were all in the habit of testing his knowledge.

"Alex, do you know how to spell wood?" asked Harry.

"Sure, Dad," said Alex confidently. "W-O-O-D."

"That's right," said Harry. "Well done."

After a while, Alex asked him again, "Dad, do you want to play?"

"No, I need to get this done," he said, as he pounded the wedge into another log.

After a while, we were distracted from watching Harry split log after log, so Alex and I went inside. Mom poured us each a glass of milk, and we sat down at the kitchen table. All three of us just gazed out the window and watched him work. It was a three-step process. First, he would stand over the log and tap the sledge onto the head of the wedge, driving the tip of the wedge into the wood. Then he would back up and give the wedge a firm smack so that it stuck in the log. Finally, he would grab the sledgehammer by its handle with his hands apart, and as he raised it in a circular motion behind him, his top hand would slide down the ash handle of the sledge next to his other hand, and he would rise up on his toes, only to bring it crashing down on the wedge in an attempt to split the log with one stroke. Sometimes that's all it took.

"Wow, Dad's really strong," Alex said.

"He's really working hard," I added.

"Your father loves to be outside, and he really enjoys the work," said Mom.

"He loves to work," said Alex. "It's all he does."

Mom asked, "So, Alex, do you know how to spell work?"

"Sure, Mom. W-O-R."

"Aren't you forgetting a letter?" prompted Mom.

"No, I don't think so. In this family, it seems that *work* never ends."

***

Choose a job you love, and you will never have to work a day in your life.
—Confucius

The harder you work, the luckier you get.
—Gary Player

Harry builds the sandbox in Roxbury

Play

Harry worked hard and played hard. He loved the outdoors, he loved to hike, and he learned from Mom to love fly-fishing. But the times when he was most playful were when he pretended to be "Wylie Coyote," an imaginary Cy Young Award-winning pitcher for his favorite baseball team, the former New York Giants (now the San Francisco Giants, a move for which he never really forgave them). I can't remember how he came up with the name, other than it was probably his favorite cartoon character, based on all the stories we told him about the crafty coyote. Harry loved the word *crafty*.

In my mind, I can see Harry take the mound, playing the part of Wylie Coyote. Behind him lay the vast expanse of green between the mound and the "Gray Monster," a battered and weathered wooden plank fence bordering deep left field of the Roxbury little league field. The game was always the same. Harry—or should I say Wylie Coyote—would take the mound and stare Alex and me down as we tried to hit the best stuff that Wylie could muster. Of course, Wylie had an all-star laden imaginary lineup supporting him in the field. Alex and I would need to hit a line drive or a hard, well-placed ground ball to get credit from Wylie for a hit. If we ever hit the ball into the outfield, we really needed to nail it. If the fly ball was too lofty, Wylie would simply pronounce, without hesitation, in sandlot baseball slang, "Can of corn, you're out!"

"Come on, that was in the gap!" I would scream from home plate.

"Ahhh." Wylie would sigh and smile. "But my center fielder is very fast." Our protests would always be ignored, but that was obviously part of the game as well. Perhaps there was a deeper lesson that life is not fair. Sometimes you hit the ball well, and you're still out. At the time, we didn't realize it, but he was teaching us that life, like baseball, is a game of inches. The little things matter, and sometimes the breaks just don't fall your way.

"But there's no way the center fielder could have caught that ball," I continued to protest.

"He got a great jump on it because he knew that you were going to pull the inside pitch."

Inevitably, I would stop whining, as I knew it was futile. Wylie had won the Cy Young Award for a reason. Wylie was the judge, the jury, and the executioner. His rulings were never overturned. He wanted us to understand that at any time, you can be an inch away from being the hero or being the goat. He was teaching us passion for a great game that he had loved since he was a boy. At his core, in many respects, Harry never really grew up.

Eventually, after several innings, it was Wylie's turn at bat. He relished his one inning. We would gather all the balls in the bag, and I would do my level best to strike out old Wylie. He always had his eye on the Gray Monster in left field. Many times, he would hit a line shot that would take one bounce to get to the fence. More than a few times, he hit balls over the Gray Monster, and he would take the patented Wylie Coyote home run trot, wearing an ear-to-ear grin that I remember to this day.

Harry loved the Giants, and he would have loved the Internet. After the New York Giants became the San Francisco Giants, he would look at the box scores in the newspaper each morning, and more often than not, the Giants' results would not be in there because of the time difference on the West Coast. He would grumble, frown, and say, "Damn it," under his breath. To Harry, the Internet would have meant instant 24/7 access to the Giants' stats.

Now when I visit the Little League field in Roxbury, which lies behind the fire station and town hall building, I am amazed at how small it seems. I still visit the field regularly. I visit my dad there, where he is buried just beyond the "Gray Monster," in the small town cemetery. I like to think of him now as being in a perpetual "Wylie Coyote" home run trot.

***

Surround yourself with people who take their work seriously, but not themselves, those who work hard and play hard.
—Colin Powell

Tragedy

On a beautiful summer evening, Carol and George Ward hosted a fun family party. The screened-in porch of their house was crowded. Kids were running around, George Ward was pouring cocktails, and the adults were consuming them. Harry enjoyed a good party, and people enjoyed being with him. His laugh was infectious, and it attracted and energized people.

I was seven and Alex was three. We were close enough in age to be rivals, yet far enough apart that not many things were truly competitive. The porch of the Wards' house overlooked the swimming pool that was on the other side of the driveway. The pool was about forty yards away from the porch and nestled in a clearing next to a big red barn. There was a weathered post and rail fence surrounding the swimming pool, with green wire fencing nailed up to the inside of the fence to ensure that small children were not able to enter the pool area.

The Wards did not have any small children, so they were not on the lookout for children around the pool. I was playing Wiffle ball on the lawn by the house. With each swing, I tried to crush the ball over the fence on the other side of the lawn away from the pool so that I could enter my own version of the Wylie Coyote home run trot. Somehow, the gate to the fence around the pool opened. Perhaps Alex opened it by himself. Perhaps one of the older kids playing tag opened it and forgot to close it. Perhaps it had never really been closed. I am not sure how it happened, but I will never forget the piercing sound of my mother's scream when someone noticed a small child floating on the surface of the pool. It was Alex.

I saw a blur of action as my mother bolted through the screen door and raced across the driveway and through the gate. Right behind her was Mr. Ward, the host of the party. Mom dove into the pool, and I remember that it seemed as if she were flying through the air parallel to the ground for quite a while before splashing into the water. I remember thinking that I was watching a superhero. My eyes were fixated on the pool in fascination, with the fear that Alex could be dead, and without thinking about it, my feet sprinted down the hill, across the driveway, and through the gate to the pool.

Mom scooped up Alex in her hands and immediately swam him to the side of the pool, where our host took him and gave him CPR and mouth-to-mouth resuscitation. His face was blue. The problem was that nobody knew when he had fallen in the water. It could have been ten seconds or ten minutes.

Harry had been inside saying good-bye to the hostess. When he arrived at the pool, I remember seeing his face. He was scared. It was the first time I had ever seen Harry look helpless. The guests of the party gathered around to watch, waiting to see if the host could bring Alex back to life. Within a few seconds, Alex sputtered up some pool water and began crying. The look of helplessness disappeared from Harry's face, and he leapt into action. "Martha and Sherman, get Alex in the car!"

Soaking wet, Mom carried Alex, now wrapped in a towel, to the car. Mom got in, clutching the little bundle, and I jumped in the backseat with her. Harry got behind the wheel and gunned the engine. Alex was still crying as we raced down the road. Harry's rough handling of the steering wheel made the tires squeal at every turn on the narrow country road. The nearest hospital emergency room was about twenty minutes away, but we were there in ten.

After Alex and Mom went behind the hospital's big double doors with the doctor, Harry and I sat together in silence for a while. I am sure that he said something to me, but I only remember sitting there in silence. After a while, Harry got up and paced the floor. He seemed to become lost deep in thought, until he realized that I was watching him intently, and then he would tousle my hair and tell me everything was going to be okay. I knew enough to know that he was saying positive things for my benefit. We both knew that everything might *not* be okay.

When the doctor finally came out, he took Harry aside, and they talked in hushed tones, the dreadful adult tones when people don't want a child to hear what they are saying. I looked away from them, but I strained my ears to pick up what they were saying. "Mr. Baldwin, it looks like Alex should be fine. It appears that he held his breath, and so he actually didn't take in that much water. However, we would like him to spend the night so we can observe him."

Harry called the Wards to let them know all was well. Mom decided to stay the night in the hospital so that if Alex woke up, he would see a familiar face. Harry and I went home quite late. We were both exhausted. He put me to bed, but within minutes, I walked down the hall into my parents' bedroom, where he was already in bed, and I asked him if I could sleep in his room that night. It was not a night for either of us to be alone. He lifted up the covers, and I crawled in beside him. "Dad, were you scared today?" I asked.

Harry paused, and then he sighed. Then with great honesty, he said, "I don't think I have ever been more scared." Even though I always took comfort in my dad's strength, I took great comfort that night in our shared sense of fear and in the vulnerability he risked by being honest with me. His honesty made me appreciate even more our shared love for my little brother and our family.

***

There's no tragedy in life like the death of a child. Things never get back to the way they were.
—Dwight D. Eisenhower

17

Value

The first family car that I remember clearly was a white 1962 Ford Torino station wagon. Over the years, it provided a great object lesson for me on Harry's view of the value of a dollar. Mom and Dad always bought each of their cars outright rather than taking out a loan. The idea of leasing a car had not really come along in the 1960s, but even if the option had been available, they were right that the best way to buy a car was to pay for it all up front, and then drive it as long as possible before it fell apart. This was the best economic approach, because as I learned from Harry, cars are depreciating assets.

The first trip to Mr. Ding's junkyard was after a little fender bender had caused the Torino's tailgate to rust out. When Mom received a small check from the man responsible for the accident, Mom used it to take Harry out to dinner rather than fix the dent. As a result, the dent festered and started to rust. Mr. Ding was able to supply us with a used white 1962 Ford Torino tailgate that had worked well for several years. However, Mom drew the line when the footwell on the passenger side of the Ford began to rust out and, through the small holes in the floor, she could see the road whizzing by under her feet as we drove along.

"Harry, I can see the road below my feet," my mom would say.

"That's not the road," Harry would say. Since he never sat in the passenger seat, he found it hard to believe that the road was visible.

"I know the road when I see it," stated Mom with confidence. "That's it. We need a new car." When Mom was emphatic about something, Harry usually knew that it was futile to ignore the issue. So, in 1972, after driving the Ford Torino hard for ten years, Mom finally convinced Harry to take the Ford to the junkyard for the second and final time.

18

Harry felt satisfied that he had come close to squeezing every last bit of utility out of the car, and that it was finally time to sell it to Mr. Ding for junk. The next weekend, Harry was upset to see that Mom had filled the car up with gas, because there was a gas crisis at the time, and the price of gas was extremely high. There were long lines at the pumps, and it cost nearly twenty dollars to fill up the Torino. In 1972, that was a lot of money. Resolved to the Torino's fate, Mom and Alex jumped in the new Chevy Malibu station wagon, and Harry and I drove in the Torino to Mr. Ding's junkyard.

The junkyard was exactly what one would imagine a junkyard to look like. There was a tall chain-link fence surrounding a rambling patch of property, with cars, tractors, motorcycles, appliances, and various forms of machinery strewn about the dirt in seeming disarray. In the center of it all was a small trailer, where it appeared that Mr. Ding lived.

In the background was the incessant barking of Mr. Ding's dog which was not all that big, but he was a feisty little mutt. I remember Mr. Ding as a wizened old codger, somewhat bent at the waist with age. He wore small wire-rimmed glasses and a baseball cap that was so old and dirty with grease stains that you couldn't make out the logo anymore.

Harry tried valiantly to barter with Mr. Ding, starting with a price of two hundred dollars. Mr. Ding sized up the situation quickly and clearly knew that with the wife and two kids waiting to go home in the new car, Harry had a weak negotiating position. Mr. Ding held firm to his offer of twenty-five dollars. I remember Harry's last pitch to Mr. Ding. Harry said, "But the car has a full tank of gas. That alone is worth twenty dollars."

"I know," said Mr. Ding. "Twenty-five dollars. Take it or leave it." Harry took it and left Mr. Ding's junkyard frowning.

"So what did you think of the junkyard?" Harry asked me as we drove home.

"It was pretty junky, I guess. I don't know."

"You're right about that," Harry conceded. "I sure learned a lesson today."

"What did you learn?" asked Mom.

"Never bring your new car and your family to the junkyard when you're negotiating the value of an old car," said Harry, with what looked to me like a respectful smile on his face as he thought about Mr. Ding.

***

Price is what you pay. Value is what you get.
—Warren Buffett

Quality

After we sold the white Ford Torino to Mr. Ding's junkyard, Harry bought a brand-new 1972 Chevy Malibu station wagon in a bronze color. At the time, our family was quite proud to own such a nice car.

One day, a stray nail happened to get stuck in our tire while driving. When we woke up the next morning, the car had a flat tire. Although Harry was annoyed at having a flat tire, he was somewhat excited about being able to show his sons how to jack up the car and change it. He called Alex and me to come outside so that we could learn how to change a tire in record time.

"When I was driving across the country to work out West during the summer in college, I had lots of flat tires. I got darn good at changing them. I got it down to less than five minutes," he said with pride.

"Five minutes is a long time," observed Alex.

"Not for a tire change," insisted Harry.

"Well, how fast will you change this tire?" I asked.

"I'm out of practice, but certainly in no more than ten minutes." Once his speech was completed, he opened the back hatch of the Malibu and got to work. Alex and I offered to help. Harry said something that, as a father, I know I have said on many occasions: "This is a dad job. You should just watch for now, and I'll let you know when you can help."

Harry proceeded to open the plastic cover along the side of the "way back," the factory-designed cargo space behind the backseats of the station wagon, where the jack and tools were located. In an orderly fashion, he pulled the jack out of a tight-fitting package from the factory. Jack designs had clearly evolved since Harry had last changed a tire, and he soon seemed confused. The pieces were clearly not intuitive to

21

him, so he needed to go over the owner's manual to figure out how the pieces plugged together in order to form the jack. Harry's frustration level began to grow as he realized that his two sons were watching him in his confusion. Alex and I shortly became bored and wandered off.

Harry kept working diligently on this problem for several hours, getting more and more frustrated. One tool broke in his strong grip as he forced it to work. Finally, he'd replaced the flat tire with the spare, but he was at his wit's end. He put the jack back into the small space in the side panel of the car." By this time, out of respect for our father, we had come back to watch him finish off the job.

This final exercise proved to be the straw that broke Harry's back. Fitting the jack, the tire iron, and the various tools back into the confined space was like a Rubik's Cube. Everything had to be in just the right place in order for the plastic panel to close fully and for the latch to shut. Finally, in a frustrated fit while banging on the panel, he shouted, "Cheap piece of shit! I'd like to see the CEO of General Motors do this." Then he turned to us and said, "Boys, remember that if a job is worth doing, it is worth doing right."

As a businessman, this quote has stuck with me over many years, whenever I am faced with an issue of quality. Do things right the first time and pay attention to the details.

**

The quality of a person's life is in direct proportion to their commitment to excellence, regardless of their chosen field of endeavor.
—Vince Lombardi

Nature

Harry loved to kneel on the grass and plant a shrub. He liked shrubs most of all because they were tougher than flowers, and they could stand up to his strong hands. Wearing his tattered Brooks Brothers button-down shirt (that once had sported a necktie and was now frayed around the collar) and his khaki pants (of which he had two identical pairs, one dirty and one clean), he would purposefully dig the hole for the shrub. He only wore gloves in the dead of winter. He loved the fact that even as a lawyer, he had calloused palms from shoveling and chopping wood.

Within a few shovel strokes, Harry heard that metallic *clank* as the shovel's blade banged into the first rock. More often than not, the center of the hole was slightly adjusted after one or two large rocks were removed. They called it Roxbury for a reason. After removing a few large rocks from his hole, he would be sweating. As the hole would get deeper, Harry would sweat more, saying the sweat made him feel good. Eventually, the hole would be deep enough, and the dirt would be piled up alongside the edge of the hole.

The way that he would kneel before the hole always made me think of the way a devout man would kneel in church. He took his planting seriously, just the way the devout take their prayers seriously. He would place the shrub in the hole and check that its best side was facing the way he wanted it to face. Then it was time to fill in the hole.

That was the part that he always let me help with when I was little. It was a straightforward task, and I, too, loved to get my fingers in the dirt. I felt great comfort in seeing my little hands in the dirt next to his big hands. I remember seeing his large hands pushing, moving, and then finally smoothing the dirt. The dirt stuck to the hair on the back of his sweaty hands, and the dirt got jammed under our fingernails. I remember looking up at him and seeing him smile broadly. There was usually a large bead of sweat on the end of his nose. He would routinely sweat through his button-down shirts and khaki pants. The dirt would then stick to his shirt and his pants, and he would appear not as a snowman, but as a dirt man.

The garden was Harry's church. In his own way, Harry prayed in the garden every weekend to give thanks to God for the earth and its harvest. I never saw Harry pray, but I loved the way that Harry loved to garden. It was his way to find peace and quiet. We would shake our heads and realize that Harry was happiest when his hands were a foot deep in loose soil when planting a new shrub.

At the end of a long day of gardening, Harry's favorite moment of the weekend was settling into his chair on the granite terrace that he built with his own hands. He was extremely proud of the terrace, even if it was a bit bumpy and uneven. Like a jigsaw puzzle, the granite rocks were laid with painstaking care. He liked his terrace so much that he added an extension to it a few years later. It was still quite a small space, just large enough to seat our family of four comfortably.

After a busy day in the garden or in the woods, Harry would sit on the terrace, a cigar in one hand and a martini in the other. From this perch, he would watch the sunset with Mom. Sometimes they would talk, but more often than not, they would simply be together and be quiet. The sunsets melting into the ridgeline across the valley were spectacular to watch.

"Now that's beautiful," Harry would say quietly as the sun dipped below the horizon. "Would you look at that?" He was most at peace at those moments. He would smile, and we could all feel his sense of contentment.

***

Adopt the pace of nature: her secret is patience.
—Ralph Waldo Emerson

Young Harry on a hike.

Harry cooling off on a hike.

Traditions

As a father, I now clearly understand the value of traditions. When I was growing up, I knew that I liked traditions, but I don't think I fully valued them until I was old enough to remember them. Harry had several traditions, or routines, that he loved, and that we, as his children, grew to love as well.

Every spring, summer, and fall we would create a large brush pile as we cared for the land in Roxbury. There would be branches that fell in storms, branches that were pruned back, and shrubs that were pulled up to replant different plants and shrubs. Inevitably, every winter, we would have a huge brush pile in Roxbury in the woods. We would then wait for the first snowfall because that meant that it was time to have the brush fire.

During the fall, as Harry built up the brush pile, we also helped him prepare a dirt safety zone around it, as if it were a moat protecting a castle. In this case, the "moat" was protecting us and the rest of the forest from the sparks from the fire. When the first snowfall came, Harry would take us up to the brush pile to finish the preparations. We worked together to neaten up the brush pile and to make sure that it was stacked as high as possible.

"Okay, boys," Harry would say, "let's light this fire."

"Can I light it?" both of us would plead.

"No, I will get it going. I want you boys to watch for sparks and stand back." This was my least favorite part of the day because it was early and still cold, and the fire never started quickly. It always took a while to get going. "I want you boys to make sure the moat is clear around the brush pile," Harry would say. Clearing the moat took hard work. We had to rake through the snow and make sure that we raked down to the dirt.

"Isn't it good enough already?"

"No. We need to protect the woods and make sure that the fire stays contained," he said. After Harry inspected everything and made sure that there was a good layer of snow and dirt around the brush, he would light the fire. Throughout the weekend, we would tend the fire and make sure that it stayed contained and safe. In some primeval way, Harry viewed this as man controlling nature. He got great satisfaction from it, and in so doing, he taught us how to deal with something dangerous in a safe way.

Although the fire would always start slowly, it would gather power and strength as it burned. Harry kept actively patrolling the fire throughout the day. We would go and come as we pleased since we were too young to appreciate the real danger of the situation. Harry understood that the fire needed to be actively managed. He would poke the branches with a metal rake that he used to continually reshape and improve the moat around the fire.

As the fire gained intensity and the flames billowed up into the sky, Harry continued to walk and poke any branches that extended out over the moat in order to control and contain the flames. Like a military sentry on duty, Harry guarded his post and stayed alert to the potential dangers. As I watched him tend the fire, I took comfort in his strong sense of responsibility. This was his fire, and he was responsible for it. He was going to protect his family, his home, and his forest, but he was also going to make sure that the fire consumed all of the dead branches from a year of gardening, pruning, and transplanting.

The first snow not only triggered the brush fire tradition, but also various Christmas traditions. One of my favorites was reading Clement Moore's poem "'Twas the Night before Christmas" as a family on Christmas Eve. I am sure that for a few years, our parents read the poem to us, but as far back as I can remember, we all read the story together. Over the years, our pacing and timing improved so that we could all read along from time to time, reciting the parts that we knew by heart. Harry's favorite line was the reference to Santa's belly being like a "bowl full of jelly."

We had many traditions growing up: Kentucky Fried Chicken at football game tailgate parties, walks around the circle, blueberry muffins on Saturday mornings, Labor Day tennis tournaments, cider making in the fall, and watching the sunset from the terrace.

Most weekends in Roxbury, we would go for at least one long walk around the circle together as a family to stretch our legs and be together. The circle was the route defined by Welton Road, to Old Tophet Road, to Gold Mine Road, and back to Welton Road. It was exactly 3.2 miles, which I measured with Mom in the car because I wanted to know exactly how fast I could run a mile. It was more of an oval than a circle, with one of the long sides having a lower elevation than the other long side. The first part of the walk was uphill, and then we reached a long, flat part with great views. We'd then descend to our dirt road to walk back home.

We would always bring a football on our walks, and Harry would be the quarterback. Alex and I would probably cover four or five miles on the walk by continually running pass plays, with one of us covering the other. Harry had a strong arm, and to us, it seemed that he could throw the ball a mile. "Go long," he would say, as he motioned with his left arm in a pushing motion, signaling for us to run farther.

"I'm open!" I would scream, my younger brother draped all over me in tight coverage.

"Cut, move, get open!" Harry would yell back, and then finally he would zing a pass in a tight spiral right at our collective chest. More than a few times, a loud *thunk* would occur as the ball bounced off some body part. "Stone fingers!" Harry would yell. His constant refrain was, "If you touch it, you need to catch it."

"The pass was too high!" I'd shout back. The banter was always lively, and someone was always tripping or falling down, providing comic relief for the entire family.

Children love routine and the comfort of tradition. My five-year-old's eyes light up when we say we are going to make s'mores over the outside fire pit behind our house. On a cold fall or winter's night, few things are more tasty. As the name suggests, once you have had one, you always want "s'more."

I suppose such traditions create a sense of belonging and a sense of security. Children love to know that there are certain experiences that they can count on. Every family needs to create its own traditions. My wife and I have created other family traditions, such as family movie night, Sunday doughnuts, skiing, Easter egg hunts, cider making, bear hunts at Waveny, and reading "'Twas the Night before Christmas."

One of my favorite traditions, one which Harry started later in his life, was cider making. This was not one of my growing-up traditions, but it became one for my children after Harry died. My mom gave Harry a cider press for his birthday one year. It is an awkward-looking contraption, constructed of wood and iron, and it stands five feet tall and about two feet wide. Moving the press is difficult and requires two strong adults leaning it back and rolling it on two wheels located at its base. In spite of its complicated and somewhat menacing appearance, it is great fun to use, and it creates a delicious product.

First you create the mash. On the side of the cider press is a large metal wheel with a crank handle on it. Harry liked to crank the wheel smoothly and continuously, which turned a wooden cylinder inside a black metal chute. On the wooden cylinder are rows of small metal tabs raised a quarter of an inch above the surface of the wood. As apples are fed into the chute, they are crushed and smashed by the rotating cylinder with the metal tabs.

The apple mash then falls down through the bottom of the chute, into a cheesecloth type of bag that is in a wooden circular form to give it shape, just as a garbage bag in a trash can. Our kids love the mashing process, and they take turns throwing the apples into the chute and turning the crank to mash them. Although Harry never got to do this with our children, I know that he would have loved it even more with a gaggle of small kids running around the cider press.

Once the apple mash has filled up the cheesecloth in the wooden circular form, we stop mashing and start pressing. The press has a thick round wooden lid that fits exactly inside the circular wooden form. Just like a printing press from the Revolutionary War era, we then screw down a metal clamp on top of the round lid, which squeezes the cider juice through the holes in the cheesecloth and out into a wooden tray that is slightly tilted. The tray has a small notch in it on the downhill side so that the cider runs into a large bucket. The seeds, stems, and pulp are caught in the cheesecloth, and the output is simply tasty juice.

The children love the immediate gratification from their work, and they grab small Dixie cups full of cider right from the bucket under the press. When I asked my five-year-old, Shane, why he liked the cider so much, he said, "Because I can take it right from the bucket." Somehow, anything tastes better if you can dip your cup in a bucket at the source.

***

A family is a sum of its traditions. Create them and celebrate them.

Martha and Harry sitting on the terrace in Roxbury

Friendship

In our home, a small silver box always sat on the coffee table in the living room. The box was a wedding gift to Harry from the groomsmen in his wedding. The box had a unique design in that there were seven signatures etched into the silver lid. The letters were not block initials or printed; they were written in the script of each person's hand. It caught my attention because it was such a nice gift from his friends.

The names engraved in the box were familiar to me. Among the names was Ed Woodsum, who is my godfather and was the tight end on Harry's college football team. Even as a young child, I knew Harry's best friends, and they were still his best friends years later. I learned that being a good friend takes hard work. He was always there for his close friends. If it was advice, comfort, or companionship, Harry always made the time for them. He used to say, "You can count yourself as very lucky if you have a handful of friends for life."

In the writing of this book, as I talked to friends of the family to get their perspective on Harry, I heard some new stories. Even though the stories were new to me, they were filled with many common themes. One of the strongest recurring themes, though, was that Harry was a great friend. He knew how to play this role.

One time early in his marriage, he and my mom were attending a dinner party. Unfortunately, one of the guests had far too much to drink. Expounding on some topic, the drunkard began to insult one of my mom's best friends by telling her how stupid she was for saying the wrong name for the author of a famous book. For some reason, the man would not let the topic go, and he kept berating my mom's friend.

People around the table were clearly embarrassed and didn't know what to do. Several men stared at their shoes or pretended to drop their napkins so that they could avoid eye contact with the man. In contrast, Harry knew exactly what to do. Harry stood up, grabbed the man by the arm, and took him outside, where he made it abundantly clear to the man that such mean-spirited insults had no place at the dinner table.

In words and in actions, Harry valued friendship. It is said about U.S. Marines, "No better friend, no worse enemy." Harry was a former Marine Corps officer, and I think this phrase aptly describes him. I was never aware of his having an enemy, but he was certainly a great and loyal friend. Nowhere was this more evident than at my wedding, when I was fortunate enough to marry Alice Reilly Toole, the daughter of Ed Toole, one of Harry's best friends. The church and the reception were filled with family friends, many of them friends of Harry.

One of the rites of passage for me to marry Alice was to meet Mimi, who was Alice's grandmother and Ed Toole's mother. I remember driving with Alice up to Hartford to have lunch with Mimi in the dining room of Macauleys, the retirement community where she lived. Mimi was an intelligent and strong woman with a keen memory and sense of humor.

The three of us had a nice lunch and talked of many things, from family to current events to politics. I was more than a bit nervous and was on my best behavior for the matriarch of Alice's family. As we were finishing our meal, Mimi felt the need to give her blessing in some way. Even though it had been years since she had seen my father, she said, "You are like your father, Harry, and I remember that he's a nice boy." Harry's polite and kind interactions years before with his friends' parents were the foundation for Mimi's seal of approval.

At the wedding, there were not two sides of the aisle; instead, there was simply one big party. The spirit of joyous celebration was palpable as one family joined another family. This wonderful moment might never have happened if Harry did not cherish his dear friends, respect their families, and keep in touch with them.

***

There is nothing on this earth more to be prized than true friendship.
—Saint Thomas Aquinas

Ed Woodsum and Harry at a football game.

Harry and Ed Toole, proving his Army uniform still fits him.

Luck

Harry's favorite card game was Hearts. I think he learned it in college, and he loved playing it. It was the perfect game for someone like Harry, a cheerful skeptic. In the game, there are far more "bad" cards than "good" cards. As individual cards, hearts are bad and earn you negative points when you take them in a trick. A trick is the card playing term used for the collection of cards gathered by the player who follows suit with the highest value card after each player has played a card going once around the table. The ultimate bad card is the queen of spades, or the "black lady," which earns the player thirteen negative points. There is only one good card in the deck, and that is the jack of diamonds, which is worth ten positive points. This mirrors a skeptic's view of life. There is often more bad in the world than good, and you need to be on your toes to avoid danger at every turn.

There are three basic tenets of the game: (1) You must follow suit if you can; (2) You cannot lead a heart until a heart has been played; and (3) Avoid the bad cards unless you believe you can win them all. This is the delightful twist to the game. Getting all the bad cards is called "shooting the moon." I can remember nothing that gave Harry more pleasure than the handful of times he shot the moon in our family games of Hearts.

Whenever we played as a family, we all knew that he was biding his time, looking for his opportunity to shoot the moon. Most of the time, the objective of the game is to avoid the bad cards. But when someone in the game is trying to "shoot," it requires an act of community spirit to stop him. Someone must step up and take a trick with some hearts or the "black lady" in it. Once we sensed that he was trying to take tricks and run the table, each of us would publicly urge the other to step up and take the trick of bad cards on behalf of the game. "Come on, Mom," I would say, "take just one heart. Don't let him shoot the moon." Each of us would always try to hold off and make the next person be "community spirited." This intriguing social dynamic fascinated Harry.

Shooting the moon was not easy to do. It was the lone individual against the other players in the game. The high-risk strategy led to ruin more often than not. Perhaps because the rest of his life was quite conservative, Harry reveled in such risk-taking in the card game. He always wore an ear-to-ear grin when he actually shot the moon.

I also loved that turn of phrase, "shooting the moon." It connotes the ultimate long shot in a whimsical way, which has always brought a smile to my face. More than anything, the smile it brought to Harry's face was what made us all smile. Given the long odds against anyone shooting the moon, Harry was not often successful, but when he was, his glee was childlike. He would dance a little jig and keep repeating, "I shot the moon, I shot the moon." We would all try to ignore him, but his smile, laughter, and the childlike giggle of glee were too much to avoid. Days later, he would still be recounting the moment with pleasure.

As I reflect back, there is something refreshing in seeing a grown man act like a child in the moment. The pure joy and happiness in Harry's laugh gave everyone permission to find joy.

***

I'd rather be lucky, than good.
—Lefty Gomez

Manners

One of the truly great pieces of advice for life is this: "If you don't have something nice to say, then don't say anything at all." Especially today—with chat rooms, e-mail, cell phone cameras, and all other forms of electronic communication—it is important never to communicate electronically in anger. When you are angry or frustrated, your judgment is impaired, and you will often regret what comes out of your mouth or what your fingers type. At least if you are face-to-face with someone, the emotions are in the moment and not captured for posterity, the way an angry message is captured and potentially forwarded out of context in an e-mail.

In high school, Harry learned a lesson about manners the old-fashioned way. His dad took him to watch a Yale baseball game before he was to attend Yale the next fall. George H. W. Bush, the future president of the United States, was the captain of the team. Harry was hoping to play baseball in college, so he was interested in seeing the caliber of play.

Before they sat down, his father told him to be careful what he said in the stands because you never knew who was sitting next to you. George Bush proceeded to go zero for three in his first three tries at bat. Harry was about to shout something obnoxious at the batter as he stepped into the batter's box for the fourth time, but he remembered his father's advice and bit his tongue.

George Bush connected with the pitch and hit a solid line drive up the middle for a base hit. Just as soon as the ball made it through the infield, the woman sitting in front of Harry and his father stood up and screamed, "Atta boy! Way to go, George!" Mrs. Bush was very proud of her son, and Harry was happy that he had not said something negative in front of George's parents.

This story stuck in his memory, and he taught us by example that it was never good to criticize other people in public. Praise in public, and criticize in private.

***

The hardest job kids face today is learning good manners without seeing any.
—Fred Astaire

Fishing

Seeing Harry truly relax was a rare treat, but when it happened, it was memorable. It happened most often in the outdoors—more specifically, in the wilderness. Something about the wilderness made all of us relax and live in the moment. My love of the wilderness started in part because I really enjoyed watching Harry in a relaxed mood.

One of my favorite fishing holes was a place called Martha's Dam. The beaver dam was named after my grandmother, and just downstream from it was Murderer's Hole, so named because it seemed that on some mornings, fishing in that small hole was more like shooting fish in a barrel than fly-fishing. After a few hours of fishing, we would make a small campfire and cook some of the brown, rainbow, and speckled trout that we had caught. The black cast-iron pan that we used would sizzle with the bacon that we cooked first to add a little grease to the pan. Once the grease was hot, we would fry up the trout. I don't think I have since had trout that tasted as good.

One morning at Martha's Dam, Harry was frustrated by seeing trout rising in the water just beyond where he could cast from the shore. He started to think about how to solve the problem. The first move he made was to take his shoes off and roll up his trousers so that he could walk gently into the lake and cast his fly out farther into the water.

This conservative approach to wading was not successful, though, and he continued to be exasperated by the trout rising just beyond his cast. He came back to the shore, and I remember that he opened his little backpack and took out a green poncho he had in case it rained. My mom said to him, "Harry, it is beautiful out here. Why are you putting on your poncho?"

He simply smiled and donned the poncho. "I've got a plan," he said with a crafty grin. As soon as the poncho was on, his pants and underwear came off. This was indeed a bold move. There he was, naked under his poncho, wading into the lake to catch the little fish that were taunting him. We all stopped what we were doing and walked over to watch him. His green poncho floated around him, up to his chest, as he cast out to where the fish were jumping.

"Dad, you're going to scare those fish," I called to him.

He laughed a deep belly laugh as he cast his fly. He was quite successful with his unorthodox fly-fishing approach. He was willing to be bold, and it worked.

***

Be bold.

Negotiation

Most Saturday mornings, my mom would cook blueberry muffins for our family of four. It was uncanny that Mom never was able to make the batter fit into muffin cups to serve eight or twelve muffins. The batch was always indivisible by four.

Mom's muffins were delicious. When they came out of the oven, they were warm, golden brown, and soft on the inside. The results of this baking inequity were fervent negotiations every Saturday morning, which often nearly led to fisticuffs between Alex and me.

One morning, when Alex and I were screaming at each other about who was going to get the last two muffins, which of course were different sizes, Harry solved the problem demonstrating his wisdom. He took out a knife, handed it to Alex, and said, "You cut, and Sherman chooses."

This concept stunned Alex and me. We realized that Harry had elegantly aligned our interests. Thereafter, whenever there was a conflict about muffins, or any other form of sharing, one brother made the division, and the other got to choose. This insured that the dividing brother would be as meticulously fair as he could be. He knew that if he wasn't, he would lose in the end.

***

Negotiate in good faith; look for the win-win solution. You cut, I choose.

Loyalty

Harry played football for Yale in the 1950s when that meant something. The Yale Bowl in those days was packed on the weekends. There was no Super Bowl; there were no multimillion-dollar contracts. The Yale-Harvard game was truly "The Game."

Things are different today, and things were different even by the 1970s and 1980s, when I was growing up. But every other Saturday in the fall, when Yale played at home, our family went to see the football game. I would sit next to Dad as he watched the game intently. He would get so emotionally involved in the game that he really did not acknowledge the presence of the rest of the family. I could see him playing the game in his mind. As he watched, he would visualize himself back in the middle of the line, with the grass between his knuckles and the dirt on his sweaty face.

I would watch his face during the plays, and he would tug and twist his lower lip in a way that evoked the intense connection that he had with the players on the field. Harry was a loyal fan not only of his college football team, but also of his favorite professional teams as well. When he was growing up, his favorite baseball team, the New York Giants, played baseball at the Polo Grounds. Bobby Thomson's walk-off home run, the "shot heard 'round the world," which won the 1951 pennant for the New York Giants, was an indelible memory of his growing up.

One of his finer moments as a baseball fan occurred one evening when I cornered him at the door when he got home. I had been studying *The Baseball Encyclopedia* all day in an effort to identify a trivia question that would stump Harry. With a grin on my face and a sparkle in my eye,

I was confident that I would stump him. "All right, Dad," I said. "I have a baseball trivia question for you. Are you ready?"

"Shoot," said Harry, as he set down his briefcase and took off his suit coat.

"When Bobby Thomson hit the 'shot heard 'round the world,' who was the runner on third base?"

Harry looked up and down. He scratched his head. And then, without hesitating, he said, "Clint Hartung was the pinch runner for Don Mueller."

"Arrrrgh!" I yelled. "I can't believe you got it." I should have known better than to ask him a question about his favorite team.

Perhaps describing passion in the context of being a sports fan might seem to cheapen the value. I hope not. Harry's loyalty to his wife, his family, and his friends was unshakeable as well. We all knew we could count on him, and we all knew that he was rooting for us, the same way that he rooted for his football team. A former Marine officer, Dad took to heart the Marine Corps motto, Semper Fidelis.

***

Be a fan of something.

Harry enjoying a football game at the Yale Bowl.

Determination

Harry waged many small battles as he expanded the boundaries of his domesticated domain in Roxbury. I likened it in my own mind to the American settlers' drive to the West, labeled Manifest Destiny by historians. Along the way, Harry encountered rocks where he wanted to plant shrubs, poison ivy where he wanted to plant flowers, and a variety of critters that seemed to revel in their ability to frustrate Harry's drive to expand his domain.

At one time, a particularly stubborn woodchuck decided to create his home under our lawn. Unfortunately for the woodchuck, he had never met a man like Harry. The woodchuck declared war by burrowing in and around a new rock garden that Harry had just created. He had taken the many rocks from the holes he had dug to plant new shrubs, and he'd formed them into a new garden, giving it a natural look and feel. As he walked around admiring his work, Harry stepped into one of the woodchuck's holes and twisted his ankle.

Harry was angered on two fronts: first, the woodchuck's digging had injured him; second, the woodchuck was a threat to his new garden. Harry set out to convince the woodchuck that there were better places to live on the property than right under his new garden.

The battle raged over several weekends. Harry would devise his plan of attack during the week, and then he would execute the campaign in typical Marine Corps fashion over the weekend. Harry first tried to flush out the woodchuck simply by putting a hose into its hole and turning on the water. He nearly emptied the well of water before he acknowledged that the woodchuck had burrowed in such a way as to create a relief tunnel for water so it would not rise and force the woodchuck's exit.

The next frontal assault was with smoke bombs purchased at the local supply company. This was exciting. Of course, as two young boys, Alex and I were eager to participate in anything having to do with a bomb, or a possible explosion. Harry said it was too dangerous, though, and not knowing what would happen, he had us stay in the house with Mom as he approached the woodchuck's hole with the smoke bomb.

We watched intently from the window as Harry knelt down, lit the smoke bomb, and placed it in the hole. Obviously thinking that there might be a real explosion, Harry hustled back toward the house. When the result was a muted "boom" and an unimpressive little puff of smoke, we all giggled at Harry's attack on the woodchuck. I am sure that the woodchuck was probably long gone before the smoke bomb went off in his hole.

Harry declared victory and threw out the remaining smoke bombs because it was clear to everyone that the word would spread within the woodchuck community that Harry's garden was not a good place for a woodchuck to make a home.

***

Don't underestimate your opponent.

The Value of a Dollar

Harry was not an intellectual, but he was well educated and wise. My grandfather liked to refer to him as a "man of action." Harry loved and respected the feeling of a hard day's work. Yet he also made it clear to us growing up that education deserved equal, if not greater, respect.

In the stories that he told as we grew up, it seemed that the age at which he had his first tough job got younger over the years, but he certainly did value those early experiences. Growing up with Harry was fun because of the stories. He'd worked on an oil rig in Texas, and he told us, "You needed to kick the pipes before you picked one up to make sure there were no snakes curled up inside." Such a comment was always followed by a grimace. We all knew that Harry hated snakes.

He wanted me to appreciate the difficulties of manual labor as an honorable way to make a living, and to appreciate the people who earned a living that way every day. While he believed there was great nobility in a hard day's work, he also hoped that I might understand that there were less exhausting ways to make a living and support a family. He understood that education was going to be critical for his children's success, and he pushed us hard so we'd understand and appreciate all forms of working.

Right up until the year that he died, Harry mowed the lawn in Roxbury. The Lawn-Boy lawnmower was a gas-powered push mower. It was quite good exercise to push the lawnmower all over the expansive lawn in Roxbury. When I was growing up, it was one of my first jobs where I started to gain an appreciation for the value of a dollar. Dad paid me minimum wage, and it took me about two hours to complete the job. During the summer, when the grass was growing quickly, sometimes I needed to mow the lawn two times within the week in order to keep it looking good. Harry liked the fact that I was earning money and working hard to do it. He wanted his sons to understand the value of a dollar and understand that manual labor is a good and noble thing.

Harry kept pushing the "wilderness" farther back away from the house, and every year it seemed that the job of mowing the lawn took longer and longer. Eventually, it was taking me well over three hours to complete the job. My mom suggested to Dad that it might be time to get a riding mower to help make the job more manageable.

Harry agreed to go look at riding mowers. He also pointed out that my younger brother, Alex, was just about to turn twelve. He remembered that this was the age that I started mowing the lawn. Not wanting Alex to miss out on the great experience, Dad came home from the store with a second push mower.

From there, my work experiences moved on to painting horse fences with creosote, leading to my first real summer job for a local general contractor, where I not only learned construction, but also all the unpleasant jobs that always go to the new guy.

The worst by far was insulating attics in August. I will never forget strapping on goggles and a flimsy little mask to prevent me from inhaling the insulation, and then climbing a ladder to the large attic of the local bookstore. The job was to start at one end, holding a hose and directing the spray of insulation all over the attic. The temperature was easily over one hundred degrees, and as my pores opened, I sweated profusely. The insulation began to stick to my drenched body. After more than an hour of this task, I emerged looking like a life-size fuzzy gray Muppet. After enjoying a good chuckle at my expense, my fellow workers swatted me with brooms to knock the insulation off me. While I valued the experience, and I have great respect for everyone who puts in a hard day's work, I realized quickly that I didn't want to be doing that kind of work every day of my life.

When Harry would raise his eyebrows at the lowest grade on a report card, Mom was always quick to point out that his grades were never as good. Perhaps that was a regret of his as an adult, that he hadn't applied himself as much as he should have in school. Whatever the reason, he always set a very high bar for Alex and me in our academics, and I think that always inspired us to reach for our full potential. What he cared about in particular was that we always worked hard and committed ourselves to giving our best efforts.

***

Other than love, the greatest gift you can give your children is an understanding and an appreciation for a job well done.

Earning

It seemed that Harry was always telling stories about adventures he'd had when growing up. He was particularly fond of telling stories of hard work out West. One of his first summer jobs was in Montana on a sheep ranch. A friend of his father owned the ranch, and he agreed to have Harry come out to work as a ranch hand. It was 1951, and Harry was a strapping twenty-year-old college football player. At ten dollars per day, Harry felt that the ranch owner was getting a great deal.

After two weeks of hard work on the ranch, Harry had blisters on his hands and his feet, but he had gained a new appreciation for the definition of a day's work. The one job that he recounted in gory detail was the hard and dirty work of shearing sheep. The sheep were dipped in a disinfectant chemical, and then the shearing process began. The combination of the horrible smell in a confined space; the wet, dirty wool; and the sheep, which were prone to bite and kick because they had other ideas about where they wanted to be and what they wanted to be doing, made this a backbreaking, frustrating, and difficult job. But Harry stuck with it, and he sheared many sheep in the first two weeks on the ranch. Harry actually worked so hard that he impressed the ranch owner.

At the end of a long day, the ranch owner put his arm around the young man and said, "Harry, you've been working really hard and getting lots done. I am pleasantly surprised, and I am going to give you a raise. Starting next week, I am going to pay you ten dollars per day."

"But, sir, you're already paying me ten dollars per day now," said Harry.

"Actually, your father has been paying me ten dollars per day to let you work out here. Now I am going to start paying you ten dollars per day because you are earning every penny of it."

***

There is joy in work. There is no happiness except in the realization that we have accomplished something.
—Henry Ford

Trust

I learned Harry's philosophy on trust early in life. He trusted you until you let him down. I am confident that life would have been different if I had broken that trust, but I didn't, and so our relationship only strengthened over the years. My time with my parents during my teenage years was actually relatively trouble free, because I knew that my parents trusted me, and I did not want to let them down.

Never did my parents place a curfew on me. They simply said, "Just use your best judgment and let us know where you are." I suppose parents know their children well, and they knew that this approach would work well with me. It would not be right for every child, but I hope that it will be right for my children and grandchildren.

There are many complex psychological issues at play between parent and child on the topic of trust, but at the end of the day, it is fairly simple. Keep your promises. From big to small, this is the way to lead your life. If you say you are going to do something, then do it. Harry taught me this by keeping his promises to me throughout my life. Whether it was a promise to play baseball with me on the weekend or to come see one of my important events—a game, a play, or a recital—Harry was always true to his word.

A trust-based relationship is a powerful thing in a family, in business, and in marriage. Trust makes life much easier. When there exists between two people a mutual commitment to honesty, integrity, and character, anything can be accomplished.

***

To make someone trustworthy, first you must trust him.
—Henry Stimson

Safety

One summer, our family spent some time hiking and exploring the White Mountains of New Hampshire. We planned to hike from hut to hut over the course of a week, covering much of the White Mountains Presidential Range. The idea was to visit a different hut each night, and then hike for seven to ten miles the next day. Mom had written in advance and gotten reservations for us in each of the huts. It sounded like a relaxing family vacation in the great outdoors.

On the first day, we parked our car at the trailhead and started hiking toward the Mizpah hut, the first hut along the trail. The huts were small cabins that had several bunkrooms off central living and dining areas. Each of the huts had a small crew of college students who cooked and cleaned the hut, also acting as innkeepers for hikers on the trail. After a full day of hiking—with plenty of false summits and "Are we there yets?"—we finally arrived at the Mizpah hut.

As we walked toward the hut, a scream erupted from inside. It was an angry scream of rage. Harry's face grew taut, and he told us to stay put while he investigated the situation. Before he could finish his sentence, another scream emanated from the hut, and the door was kicked open by a shabbily dressed, dirty, long-haired young man, who ran out of the hut carrying something wrapped in a blanket under his arm like a football.

"Martha, stay here with the boys," Harry said, as he walked purposefully toward the hut.

"Be careful," said Mom.

I could tell that Harry was nervous. This did not feel right. Something was wrong. More screams came from the hut. Harry entered the hut to find two young men using a rope to tie another young man to a large wooden picnic table in the middle of the hut's one main room.

The young man on the table was shouting, "Help me, help me, help!" The two culprits who were tying him up looked guilty, and as Harry entered, they acknowledged their guilt by deciding to run for it. Harry was on edge. Sensing danger, he was in a combat pose. Rather than engage the assailants, he decided to get out of their way as they fled the scene.

Harry then grabbed a kitchen knife and started to cut the ropes that bound the young man on the table. "What the hell is going on here?" he asked.

"We were just raided by the Crawford hut. They got the clock!"

"What are you talking about?" asked Harry, still not understanding the situation.

"The huts each have a mascot or a symbol. The Mizpah symbol was the cuckoo clock, and now the Crawford crew has it." We had arrived in the middle of the White Mountains' version of a hard-core, full-contact college fraternity raid.

The thing that I remember, though, is that I felt safe. Even though I was nervous, I also knew that Harry would handle the situation.

***

A father's mission is to ensure his family's safety.

Harry enjoying a short nap on a hike.

Reputation

The frightening thing about your reputation is that it takes your entire lifetime to build it, and you can lose it forever in one short minute by using poor judgment. Every day, I think about living up to Harry's high standards, and I remember the last two sentences of the eulogy that was delivered at the funeral of Sherman Baldwin, my grandfather and my namesake. One of his best friends said, "And lastly his love for his family—a love complete and true, and nearest of all to the center of his being. All in all, his qualities of mind and spirit came as near perfection as a man can come." I quoted these words at Harry's memorial service because they were equally true about him.

These words ring in my head whenever I am faced with a tough ethical decision. Whenever I am faced with the possibility of taking a shortcut, I realize that there are no shortcuts to success.

One of the human traits that separated Harry from the pack was his profound sense of fairness. Routinely, he was called into adjudicate squabbles between his partners at work or arguments at home. Everyone who came to know Harry felt that he was someone to be trusted.

My grandfather was not perfect. Harry was not perfect, and neither am I. Harry earned a reputation as a man of character by living it every day. I suppose that is as near as perfect as a human can be. Every day, one must strive to do the best one can do, in whatever the chosen endeavor, in order to honor oneself and to honor one's family name.

***

The one thing I want to leave my children is an honorable name.
—Theodore Roosevelt

Three generations: Sherman, Harry and me.

Competition

Harry loved to compete, and he loved to win. He appreciated the clarity and the simplicity of competition. Of course, it is more fun to win than to lose, but what should be celebrated is the spirit of competitiveness, the desire to strive and to win. One of his favorite games was squash. He loved the one-on-one intensity of competing in a tight space with another man. He had great ongoing grudge matches against another lawyer who was at the same skill level. Every match was tight. Some nights he would win, and some nights he would lose, but he loved competing.

This grudge match occurred once per week, and it had been going on continuously for several years when Mom finally said she would like to meet his nemesis from the squash court. She wanted to invite Harry's squash opponent for dinner. Harry admitted to the fact that he didn't even know whether the man was married. In fact, he knew precious little about his opponent because all they did was compete.

Mom dug for more information, and Harry was able to uncover the fact that his competitor was divorced. He proceeded to offer her what little description he could. Within weeks, Mom had identified a divorced woman she thought might be a good fit, based on what little she had to go on. The dinner was set up for a few weeks later.

A couple of days before the fateful night, Mom was talking to a friend, and she described the upcoming dinner party and the guest list. Fortunately, her friend informed her that Harry's nemesis had actually been married to the woman that Mom was planning to introduce to him.

"Harry, for goodness' sake, you have really messed this up!" shouted mom.

"They were already married?" said Harry sheepishly.

"You're damn right. You'd think you might have known that the man was divorced. You've been playing with him in a small court for several years."

"Sorry. I guess I should have asked, but we really just play. We enjoy the close game. We don't talk a whole lot."

"Clearly," huffed my mom, clearly dumbfounded by the lack of human insight on Harry's part.

They were able to cancel the dinner, but Mom never let Harry forget this story. Mom was mortified that he had not been able to figure this out in simple conversation with his squash opponent. Needless to say, the dinner would have been quite awkward.

It became clear to Mom that when Harry was competing, he had little time for small talk.

***

Leave it all on the field.

Fun

One of my favorite memories of Harry is of him seated at a dinner party with dear friends. He is visibly laughing, with his head tilted up and his back arched. The pure pleasure and emotional release that is expressed in every fiber of his being is fantastic. He certainly faced some tough and stressful times during his life and his career, but he knew how to laugh and how to release.

There are a few secret words and phrases that will always make Alex and me laugh. The words "Monald" and "saku," as well as the phrases "one chuck per block" and "cheap piece of shit," each have special meaning to us, evoking a story and a memory that brings a smile to each member of our family.

The "saku" story is one of my favorites. It was Christmas Eve, and we had gathered as a family with my maternal grandparents. We had created a tradition of playing a short game of charades as a family. We would divide the teams up so that each team had a member of each generation: a child, a parent, and a grandparent.

The topics were all written on small pieces of paper, which were then folded and placed in a bowl. My grandmother, whom we called Granny, drew one of the toughest of them one year. We could tell by the frown on her face that the topic was a tough one. Granny struggled to think up her approach, and then she launched into it as best she could.

Granny grabbed her right ear. "Sounds like!" we all shouted.

Then she pretended to pack a bag. "Bag ... clothes ... trip ... groceries," we guessed. Granny shook her head with disgust. She repeated her motions, and one of us yelled out "Pack!" Granny nodded enthusiastically and indicated that the word was a bit longer and somewhat different.

"Packing ... packs ... packer!" we shouted.

After several more minutes of frantic guessing that led to nowhere, Harry finally blurted out, "Saku!" with an exasperated yell. It sounded like a samurai warrior's final scream. We all stopped playing and looked at him.

"What the heck is a saku?" I asked Harry. From that moment on, Granny had a new nickname. Every Christmas Eve, Harry, her irreverent son-in-law, would recall that infamous charades game and refer to her as "Saku."

Granny had the last laugh on the following Christmas. Although she was a dear woman, Granny was not very good at charades. She was given the topic word "honey." It just so happened that Honey was the name of our dog, a wonderful, loving mutt and a beloved member of the family. After reviewing the topic and pondering it, Granny smiled, as if confident in her ability to nail this one quickly. Dad had just returned from the kitchen with a fresh cup of coffee, and he said, "All right, Saku, we're ready to guess. Let's have it."

As soon as Harry sat down, Granny dropped to her knees and charged his chair on all fours, acting like the family dog in an attempt to have her team guess the word honey in record time. In her enthusiasm to act the part, Granny pawed aggressively at Harry's leg. In surprise at the sight of his mother-in-law on all fours, he spilled his hot coffee in his lap, and he shrieked, "Sak-uuuu!" at the top of his lungs.

Granny was shocked. Dad was hopping around the living room, and the entire family was rolling on the floor in laughter.

***

Most people are about as happy as they make up their minds to be.
—Abraham Lincoln

Harry at dinner with friends.

Harry and his mother in law Martha Denniston

Laughter

Harry loved to laugh, and his laugh was deep, heartfelt, and infectious. Countless family meals in our home were dominated by long, loud fits of laughter as we shared stories and jokes with each other. Many of the pictures in our photo albums of Harry were of him laughing from somewhere deep in his belly. His laugh shook his body and made others laugh with him.

During one family dinner, in a dimly lit and normally quiet French restaurant, we were all laughing hysterically. When the main course arrived, our boisterous behavior was interrupted by a man who walked out of the shadows from the other side of the restaurant. He extended his hand to Harry, saying, "You must be Harry Baldwin, Yale class of nineteen fifty-three. I'd recognize that laugh anywhere." He had not seen my dad in over thirty years, since they had graduated from Yale, but he knew there was only one man who could laugh like Harry.

***

Aspire to be known for your laugh.

Roughhousing

Children are like puppies. They wrestle, roll, gouge, tickle, squeeze, bite, and smush each other, giggling while they're doing it. While we watch our children roughhouse, Alice and I simply pour each other another glass of wine and smile at each other as they roll and tumble across the floor, laughing and giggling until the inevitable tears put an abrupt end to the tussle. Alice rolls her eyes in the same way that my mom did when Harry, Alex, and I would start roughhousing.

One of our favorite family traditions from growing up with Harry was the concept of "one chuck per block." This was loosely based on the notion that the defending cornerback in football was only legally allowed to hit the receiver within five yards of the line of scrimmage. This was the defender's one free "chuck."

One evening, as we walked fifteen to twenty blocks back to our apartment after a nice family dinner, everyone was allowed one chuck per block, with the understanding that Mom was off limits, if you knew what was good for you. Alex and I started to "chuck" each other as we walked down the street. Alex bided his time, looking to take Harry by surprise. He was looking for an opportunity, and he found it.

After both Alex and I had "chucked" Harry early on in the block, we realized that we were only one block away from our street. Alex lagged behind him as we neared the right turn onto our street. After we turned the corner, Alex, considering it a new block even though we had not crossed a street, came up from behind Harry and laid a good chuck on him, nearly knocking him over. Harry quickly regained his composure as Alex sprinted to escape to our building down the street. "I'm going to get you, you little bugger" were Harry's last words as he sprinted down the sidewalk after my little brother.

Harry still had some speed, and Alex had underestimated the old man. Dad was gaining on Alex as they neared the awning of the building. However, Alex was wearing sneakers, and he was able to cut sharply into the building. When Harry tried to stop, his leather-soled shoes hit a patch of black ice, and his feet slipped out from under him. He flew by the entrance to our building in a horizontal manner, completely parallel to the ground. Groaning, he skidded to a stop on his back. I remember seeing a neighbor simply watch dad fly by as he held the door open. "Good evening, Harry," he said.

***

Families that roughhouse together, stay together.

Harry and his two boys.

Humor

Harry was a member of the board of trustees for the New York Botanical Garden, one of New York's most beautiful attractions. There are spectacular flowers, trees, and now there is even an azalea walk that was named after my grandfather and father, who both contributed a great deal of time and energy to build one of the country's greatest botanical gardens.

In the 1970s, the botanical garden was looking to build a new modern arboretum, and Harry was one of the board members tasked with raising the money to do so. Harry set up an appointment with an elderly woman in her Park Avenue apartment one afternoon. Another board member joined him for support. It was a huge project, and they were going to ask this woman to donate a great deal of money.

The other board member happened to be a woman who was friendly with the potential donor. When Harry was shown into the sitting room, he saw that his colleague from the board was already seated comfortably on a substantial sofa against the far wall. The butler gestured for Harry to sit on a small Louis XV chair in the middle of a beautiful Oriental carpet. Harry was a large man, and he was nervous about the idea of sitting on the antique, but he also did not want to appear rude … so he sat down on the chair.

He did so as gently as he could, but as soon as his bottom touched the beautiful silky fabric of the chair, physics took over. The chair collapsed under his weight, and it splintered into a dozen pieces, which scattered about the oriental carpet. Harry was flat on his back, wriggling around like a beached whale, when the lady of the house made her entrance.

71

In an attempt to minimize the damage, Harry's fellow board member addressed the hostess by saying, "How good to see you. By the way, I know a wonderful craftsman who could fix this chair." While his colleague was trying to make the best of an awkward situation, Harry was simply trying to stand up under the stern gaze of the chair's owner.

"You must be Harry Baldwin. So nice to meet you," she said coolly.

"It's a pleasure to meet you," uttered Harry, quite embarrassed by the situation. "I am terribly sorry about the chair. Of course I will get it repaired."

"Mr. Baldwin, it is not the first time that chair has been broken, but I do believe it is the last." She smiled, breaking the tension with her sense of humor, and then she agreed to write the large check needed for the new arboretum.

Whenever I visit the arboretum, I grin as I think about my dad lying on his back amidst the splintered remnants of the antique chair on the floor of a luxurious Park Avenue apartment.

***

Common sense and a sense of humor are the same thing, moving at different speeds. A sense of humor is just common sense, dancing.
—William James

Marriage

Harry expected a lot from his children. I think it came from the fact that his father had probably expected a lot from him. However, there was never any doubt in my mind that he loved me. I actually only remember him saying the words once or twice in my life. Fathers just did not say "I love you" when I was growing up. Yet when he put his arm around me or simply patted me on the back, I knew that he was proud of me and would love me no matter what. This alone gave me great confidence.

The best lesson that I learned from Harry about love and marriage when I was growing up was observing how much he loved my mom. They had been married for thirty-five years when he died from Lou Gehrig's disease in 1997. They'd had their arguments and their ups and downs, but there was never any question about the deep love and fondness that they shared for one another. One of the arguments that they had, which dragged on for quite a while, was about the wallpaper for the dining room in Roxbury. After months of arguing back and forth, I came home to see that the compromise was white wallpaper with a barely perceptible pattern on its surface. Alex and I laughed at this "great compromise" for years.

Such arguments were usually about silly things, and they were relatively rare. Over the years of marriage, Harry became quite dependent on Mom, and on too many occasions took her for granted. However, when Mom once became quite ill, it was amazing to see how quickly he was able to change and focus on her needs. I had never before seen Harry wash the dishes, do laundry, or clean house. But he did what needed to be done and cared for my mom over the course of several months until she recovered. He loved her deeply.

Prolonged illness can put stress on a family and can sometimes break families apart. In our case, at that time, it probably brought us closer together. The sad thing is that it took mom's illness to change Harry's behavior. The good thing was that he did; the bad thing was that he needed to.

***

The whole purpose of a husband and wife is that when hard times knock at the door you should be able to embrace each other.
—Nelson Mandela

Harry, Alice, Sherman, Martha and Alex having fun at our wedding.

Martha and Harry on their wedding day.

Integrity

Harry always tried his best to do the right thing. He was a simple man and therefore believed that if you were always honest, it never got confusing since you always told the truth. He always did the right thing, even when nobody was watching.

There are many examples of when he taught me about integrity, honesty, and character, but this one is my favorite. We had just finished construction on a renovation to our home in Roxbury. The final step was for the flooring team to come sand down the oak flooring and then apply a couple of coats of polyurethane.

After preparing and finishing the floor, a worker decided to light a cigarette a little too close to the highly flammable polyurethane. A bad fire started. Fortunately, the fire department was able to put it out before major structural damage was done, but anyone who has lived through fires knows that the worst part is the smoke damage.

Even though the damage was not too extensive, many things of value were destroyed, and many others damaged by the smoke. It was clear to Harry that he would actually need to file an insurance claim. This was extremely upsetting to him. He felt that insurance was something that you needed to have but should never use. In his way of thinking, if you actually used it, then your premiums would increase, and it would be more expensive on a recurring basis. He tried to talk Mom out of filing a claim, but Mom fortunately prevailed, and they decided to file a claim for the first time in their married life.

It was stressful preparing for the claims officer's visit. Harry got out his trusty yellow legal pad and his number two pencil and went through everything meticulously with Mom. He wanted to get it right. When all was said and done, he had a significant stack of yellow pages that he and Mom had worked on together for several days. They had done their best to estimate the replacement value for the long list of possessions.

When the claims officer arrived, the family was tense. Mom and Dad invited the man into the dining room, where they sat down together. After some initial sympathetic comments by the insurance man, as well as some other pleasantries, Harry slid the stack of yellow papers across the table to the insurance man. The man looked at the first page for all of ten seconds before saying, "Mr. and Mrs. Baldwin, your claim request is approved in full. I am very sorry for your loss and inconvenience."

I could tell that Harry was surprised. He had been expecting a long inquisition and a serious study of each line item. "Thank you, but do you mind telling me why? You've barely looked at the first page."

"Mr. Baldwin, I have been doing this job for twenty years, and I've never seen anyone claim a Kodak Instamatic camera. Usually people claim that they have lost Nikons or Leicas. Clearly, you are an honest man, and I am sure that follows through the rest of your claim."

***

No legacy is so rich as honesty.
—William Shakespeare

Glory Days

When Harry was sixteen, he graduated from high school. While he was
a bright young man, he graduated so young not because of any particular
brilliance, but because his parents had simply started him quite early
in school. At any rate, Harry's parents decided that he was too young to
go to college right away, and that he needed a change of environment
and another year to mature. So, in a dramatic move, they shipped Harry
off to Scotland to attend Edinburgh Academy for a postgraduate year of
schooling.

Harry had been quite a good football player in high school, and even
though he was young, he was big and strong. When he got to Scotland,
he realized that rugby was the closest thing he would find to football,
and so he learned to play. Needless to say, he had fond memories of his
year playing rugby in Scotland. I never truly appreciated how fond they
were until we visited Edinburgh Academy on a family vacation when I
was sixteen.

It was summertime, and of all the places to spend time on a summer
vacation, I think that visiting a school was low, if not last, on my list.
Harry, however, wanted to visit his old school and see how it had changed.
I am sure that at some point during the conversation, he reminded me in
a pointed way that he was funding the vacation.

So that decided it: we were going to visit Edinburgh Academy. I
distinctly remember the somber gray and frankly unimpressive nature
of the school as we walked through the black metal front gates. Harry
felt strongly about this place, for I could see it in his eyes. He didn't
get misty-eyed or anything, but he did stand there in the courtyard and

inhale deeply. He soaked in his surroundings and smiled. His mind seemed to race as he relived moments from his past.

I remember him muttering, "It hasn't changed at all. Thirty years, and it's all the same." As we walked across the cobblestone courtyard toward one of the administrative buildings, there was not a soul to be seen. Of course, it was the middle of summer, so we weren't expecting to see many students. We approached the gray stone building and the door opened. Out walked an elderly gentleman, who smartly stepped down the two or three steps and came face to face with our little family.

With barely a moment's hesitation, the man looked into my father's eyes and said, "Harry Baldwin, nineteen forty-nine, undefeated rugby team. Welcome back, lad."

"Why, thank you, sir," said Harry. "And you're Mr....?"

"I am Mr. Armstrong. Don't you remember me?"

"Why, of course I do," said Harry politely. My father's face broke into the broadest smile I had ever seen. Mr. Armstrong was probably the only teacher who still remained at the school from 1949, when Harry had led the team to a perfect season.

This teacher went on to tell Alex and me the story of how the team designed a trick play around the strength of Harry's arm. "You see, the team would run to the right side of the field in a deception maneuver, and then send a little winger, who hung back behind the team, racing to the left side of the field. Then Harry here would heave a long, lateral pass across the field, and the little winger would catch it and run it in for a score!" Mr. Armstrong had a huge grin on his face.

It was a moment that a father cherishes: the moment when a teenager actually looks at his father with newfound respect and admiration.

***

On rare occasion, we should all relive our glory days.

Optimism

Harry was a cheerful skeptic. He was not a glum or dark person, but he was often skeptical. I think it was the combination of Marine Corps training, followed by legal training, that cemented his skeptical view of life.

Without question, Harry's philosophy of life was summed up by Murphy's Law, which is quite simple and elegant. Murphy said, "If anything can go wrong, it will." Murphy's law originated at Edwards Air Force Base in 1949. Captain Edward A. Murphy of the United States Air Force was a flight test engineer on a project that focused on determining how much sudden deceleration a person could stand in a crash. Captain Murphy's willingness to think of all the things that might go wrong led the project to a stellar safety record. Over the years, people who ascribed to Murhphy's sense of skepticism added new corollaries to the original law.

Harry's Marine Corps training certainly was aligned with this philosophy, and it drove him to prepare in great depth for any activity because the worst often does happen. One birthday we gave Harry a small paper calendar with a different corollary to Murphy's Law for every day of the year. He would start each day with a good chuckle, and he kept many of the sayings in his dresser drawer for years. A few of his favorites are listed below:

Love: All the good ones are taken.
Technology: New systems generate new problems.
Commerce: To err is human; to forgive is not company policy.
Teaching: You never catch on until after the test.

War: Friendly fire—isn't.

Fire Brigade: If it's stupid but it works, it ain't stupid.

Photography: Autofocus—won't.

Toddler: When you forget the stroller, they will want to ride.

EMT: All bleeding stops ... eventually.

Stains: The chances of a slice of buttered toast landing buttered side down are inversely proportional to the cost of the carpet.

It is important to remember that Murphy thought of himself as an optimist.

***

Optimism is a force multiplier.
—General Colin Powell

Faith

Harry was a Christian, but he only went to churches for weddings and funerals. He believed deeply in the Ten Commandments and the Lord's Prayer, not as words to recite, but as beliefs to live by. He tried his best to lead a good life, and he did unto others as he would want them to do unto him. He treated everyone with respect, no matter whether he was the man directing traffic at the town dump or the CEO of a major corporation.

Harry viewed faith as a personal issue, and he simply had faith in himself, his family, and his friends. He did not feel the need to join a church to have this faith. He joined other organizations and contributed to different groups with his own personal approach to community service. I never really spoke to him about religion, other than to let him know that as a teenager, I got myself baptized and confirmed as an Episcopalian. For me, belonging to the larger Christian community is important, for it gives me an inner strength that I know is shared with a broader community.

When Harry was diagnosed with Lou Gehrig's disease, I leaned heavily on my faith and prayed every day for him. However, I never talked to him about how he was coping and if he was praying. Coping with something as weighty as an incurable illness demands a faith in a power greater than oneself. Harry was not a particularly religious man, but his spirit was deeper and more genuine than that of anyone I have ever known.

***

Harry would have appreciated the Ten Commandments, cowboy style. These words are written on the wall of the Cross Trails Church in Fairlie, Texas:

1. Just one God.
2. Honor yer Ma & Pa.
3. No telling tales or gossipin'.
4. Git yourself to Sunday meeting.
5. Put nothin' before God.
6. No foolin' around with another fellow's gal.
7. No killin'.
8. Watch yer mouth.
9. Don't take what ain't yers.
10. Don't be hankerin' for yer buddy's stuff.

Dreams

When Harry was in high school, he played football and baseball. He was an excellent athlete in his day. When he arrived at college, he wanted to play both sports, but he learned that there were spring football sessions in which the coach expected all of the players to participate.

The football coach was quite an intimidating man, and he made it clear that if anyone skipped the spring practices, then he would not play the following fall. Therefore, Harry decided to just focus on football and abide by the coach's desire to practice in the spring for football. He always regretted his decision to give up playing baseball.

Harry learned an important lesson from one of his good friends named Joe. Joe was probably not as good a baseball player as Harry, but Joe loved baseball—again, probably not as much as Harry. Joe loved baseball almost as much as football, so he decided that he wanted to play baseball in the spring.

Joe was an outstanding football player, even though he skipped the spring practice schedule for football and disobeyed the football coach's unwritten rule. At the end of the day, Joe was elected captain of the football team. One of the reasons was because he had the courage to do what he wanted to do, and he was passionate about every sport he played.

***

Chase your dreams and pursue your passions.

Avoid the counsel of your fears and naysayers.
—General Colin Powell

Patience

My entire family took me to college because it was only about an hour drive from our home. We packed up the station wagon in the morning, and then started driving in the late morning. Along the way, Alex complained of being hungry, and against his better judgment, Harry agreed to stop for a quick lunch at a Howard Johnson's.

We were seated in a booth, and the young teenage waitress nervously took our order. If it was not her first day, it was certainly her first week, because she was clearly not familiar with the menu. She meticulously took notes as we ordered. Harry could see that a complex order could create a significant delay, so he encouraged all of us to keep our orders simple. As a result, we each ordered a cheeseburger and fries, along with a soda.

I cannot imagine how stressed I will feel when I am taking my children to college someday, but I can appreciate how Harry must have been feeling. He was nervously tapping his fingers as we waited for our food. After we had each had a second soda, we still did not have our lunch. He was starting to fidget, and the waitress was starting to avoid our table. Something was not right. Unbeknownst to us at the time, one of the cheeseburger platters had fallen on the floor in the kitchen. The waitress, trying to abide by her training, wanted to serve our party at the same time, so three cheeseburger platters sat under a heat lamp while a new cheeseburger was cooked.

Harry was really getting antsy now. Finally, the waitress came over to our table, and I will never forget what he said. "I want to change our order. Forget the cheeseburgers. Just bring us four pieces of white toast and the check in three minutes. Can you handle that?" The young waitress ran into the kitchen to find her manager. Interestingly enough, our cheeseburgers arrived less than three minutes later.

After our lunch, as we drove away, Harry said, "I was too tough on that waitress. I guess I'm nervous about dropping you off at college."

"She'll get over it, Dad," I said.

"No, I need to be more patient. It's not my strong suit," Harry admitted.

I always found it refreshing when Harry was able to understand and see his own foible. He made me realize that a man steps up and admits to his mistakes.

***

Patience is a virtue.

Man's Best Friend

Harry loved dogs. His love for them started early in life, but he never felt more love for a dog than he did for one springer spaniel named Jesse. When I was two years old, I had a close call with a German Shepherd. We were at friends' house for the weekend, and as a small toddler, I wandered off into the field in the backyard of their home. I just kept walking, probably going after a butterfly or simply walking in a straight line because I was so impressed with my ability to do so.

The next-door neighbor had a German shepherd, which saw me wandering aimlessly in the field. Somehow able to escape from his fenced-in yard, the dog raced toward me as I toddled in the open field. While I have no recollection of this, what happened next is quite remarkable. Harry saw what was happening, and he started to run toward me, shouting in an attempt to scare off the oncoming dog. This alerted Jesse, who leapt into action and sprinted toward me. Harry was running as fast as he could, but he could not close the distance quickly enough.

At full tilt, Jesse ran past me and intercepted the German shepherd, tackling the dog with all his weight. While the two dogs growled and tussled nearby, Harry was able to pick me up and escape the scene. Jesse was then able to extricate himself with no injuries.

Who knows what would have happened, but I don't think that the German shepherd was rushing up to lick me gently on the face. I believe he saw me as a meal. Harry hugged Jesse for the rest of the day. And for the rest of his life, Jesse knew he could always count on Harry for bits of steak off his plate.

As a result, our family has always had a soft spot for dogs. While I was growing up, our wonderful mutt Honey was the ultimate adaptable animal. In the few years before he died, some of my favorite memories of Harry are of him lying on the floor with our dog Ana. He would hold her head, look into her eyes, and rub her ears. There is something special about man's bond with dogs, and Harry and I shared this love of dogs.

***

What counts is not necessarily the size of the dog in the fight—it's the size of the fight in the dog.
—Dwight D. Eisenhower

Harry, our dog Ana and me.

Martinis

I think Harry just liked the sound of the word martini. He clearly enjoyed the taste of martinis, because he had at least one every night. According to one of my favorite stories, Harry had developed this fondness early in his career as a lawyer. As a young lawyer, Harry and his colleagues would meet Friday evenings at a small Italian restaurant that valued the patronage of these hardworking young attorneys.

In an effort to blow off steam and put the frustrations of the week behind them, Harry and his young lawyer friends would put away more than a few martinis. One Friday night, their regular waiter presented Harry with the bill at the end of the evening. While he had once again had had quite a few martinis, Harry was capable of realizing that the bill was approximately twice the size of the normal Friday night bill.

"Frank, what's the deal here? This bill is about twice what it should be. Are you trying to slip one by me?"

"Mr. Baldwin, you're right. The bill is exactly twice what it should be. That's because last Friday, when I gave you the check, you signed the tablecloth."

Harry always recounted this story with a smile, and with the recognition and understanding that such behavior was inappropriate. We all make mistakes when we are young, but some mistakes should only be made once.

***

Everything in moderation.

Cigars

Harry didn't just smoke cigars; he devoured them. I don't mean that he chain-smoked them; on the contrary, he didn't even smoke every day. But when he did have a cigar, he literally devoured it. He would smoke it down to the nub, and then, from my perspective as a child, he seemed to chew on it until it disappeared. I grew up thinking he ate them.

Cigars were a noticeable part of Harry because he wore the effects of them. The chests of his sweaters had little holes in them, not from moths, but from the hot ashes of his cigars, which would tumble down his chest onto his lap. He would brush them off aggressively, but much to my mom's chagrin, the damage would be done. Rapidly, a new sweater or a new suit would be marred with the hot ashes from a crumbling cigar.

In contrast, I have never smoked anything in my life, and I attribute this, at least in part, to what Harry called "moking" (rhymes with "smoking", which was an awful form of punishment he subjected us to when we were kids. If we were misbehaving while he sat in his chair smoking his cigar at the end of the day, he would grab whichever one of us was within his reach.

When I was the unlucky one, I remember him pulling me, giggling and shrieking, toward him, like a monster hauling his prey into his cave. Once within his grasp, he would grab my ear. Then I was really in trouble. Harry had a viselike grip, and once he had my ear, he pulled my face close to his and exhaled smoke into my face.

From his perspective, "moking" us was a form of humorous punishment. It was actually quite funny when it happened to my brother, but when it happened to me, I didn't like it at all. After Harry "moked" us, he would release a big belly laugh that sounded as if he had just pulled a prank on you. But it wasn't funny as far as I was concerned. I hated those cigars, and while the cigars aren't what killed Harry, I know they were not good for him or for me.

***

Don't act up within reach of a monster with a cigar.

Charity

Harry and my mom discovered Roxbury, Connecticut, in 1969. I was only six years old, and every weekend or vacation that I had for the next eight years, and when on vacation from boarding school and college, I spent in Roxbury. A beautiful rural Connecticut town with rolling hills and open land for dairy farms, I called the place home as I grew up. Unlike most of the Northeast—and for that matter, most of the country—Roxbury is substantially still the same, over thirty-six years later. Harry is in part responsible for this fact because he helped to found the Roxbury Land Trust.

The trust started out small, with a focused mission to preserve the rural integrity of Roxbury. Harry's knowledge as a trusts and estates attorney was valued because he understood how to make land gifts a benefit to both the town and to the land donor. Over the years, the Roxbury Land Trust has created a patchwork quilt of land stitched together from a variety of land gifts across the hills and valleys of the town. Today the land trust holds over three thousand acres of land today. He received great pleasure from helping with the trust. He always felt that the mission supported his self-interest in keeping a rural setting in Roxbury, which would continue to keep it the special place that both he and Mom treasured.

Although Harry also served on various boards and parents' committees at our schools, to be involved with our education, the land trust meant the most to him. With the trust, he provided valuable services and shaped it into a healthy organization that continues to do great work today. The Baldwin Preserve is dedicated in his honor, and the mile-long trail leads through a glen of azaleas, which were some of his favorite shrubs.

Harry's involvement in the land trust was a great lesson to me. He loved to garden, and he loved the outdoors. It was his way to pursue his passion and align it with his desire to give back to the community. One should strive to be a joiner of quality organizations, and a leader within them, because life is much more fulfilling when lived in partnership with other people pursuing a common goal in the service of something larger than oneself. The land trust was lucky to have Harry's leadership and his vision, but he was also lucky to have the land trust, for the organization has given him a certain degree of immortality as it lives on.

***

If you haven't any charity in your heart, you have the worst kind of heart trouble.
—Bob Hope

Investing

In 1985, I was a junior in college, and the issue of the day was apartheid in South Africa. Apartheid was the term used to describe the segregated state in which blacks and whites lived their daily lives in South Africa. There were horrible slums called shantytowns, where the blacks were forced to live and raise their children. The government was run by a small minority of whites, who oppressed the majority of the people in the country, who were black.

Nelson Mandela, a man of tremendous character, who spent most of his adult life in prison for his belief in a desegregated and united South Africa, led a movement to end apartheid. Students who were passionate about Mandela's movement created their own shantytown on campus to protest the fact that the university's endowment owned stock and invested in companies that did business in South Africa, thereby supporting the economy of this corrupt apartheid regime. One of the companies in question was IBM.

IBM was a great company in 1985, and over twenty years later, it is still a great company. However, at the time, I felt that I needed to do something to acknowledge and protest the fact that IBM was supporting the economy in this apartheid state. So one day, I told Harry that I wanted to sell the small number of shares in IBM stock that my grandfather had given me when I was born.

"You want to do what?" said Harry, with a tone of incredulity.

"I want to sell my IBM stock." I spoke with the ignorant confidence of a twenty-one-year-old college student.

"IBM is a great company with sound financial fundamentals. You should hang onto the stock." Harry dismissed the idea completely and said that all indications were that IBM stock would continue to grow. He understood my ethical concerns, but he said that such concerns did not affect a company's stock price.

I stuck to my conviction, though, and sold the stock. Within weeks, IBM stock started a long downward spiral, for many reasons other than South Africa. As it turned out, I'd sold at IBM's peak value, which it did not achieve again for at least another seven years. At Christmas that year, I wrote Dad a short Christmas card and put it in his stocking. The card quoted Winston Churchill, who once said, "If a man is not liberal at the age of twenty, he has no heart; and if he is not conservative by the age of forty, he has no brain."

Later that year, as IBM stock continued going down, Harry wrote me a nice conciliatory note about investing, in which he asked me for some "ethical investing tips" because his portfolio of "sin stocks" was not doing very well. IBM was obeying the law at the time, and protesters were simply seeking to change the law. Unethical and unlawful actions can have a great impact on a company's value. Warren Buffet, one of the greatest investors of all time, warns the CEOs of his companies that the five most dangerous words in business are "Everybody else is doing it." This is why character is important. Just because other people are doing something does not make it right.

As we later learned with the Enron scandal in 2001, the unethical actions of its management team destroyed the company and cost its investors billions of dollars. Clearly, the ethics of a company's management do affect value. At the end of the day, I try to buy stock in a company that has strong financial fundamentals, competent and ethical leadership, strong prospects for growth, and for some reason, is undervalued by the market.

I learned a little bit about investing from this experience with Harry, but more than anything else, I learned that it is acceptable to disagree with your father and be your own person, as long as you do it with respect. In this case, I was fortunate with the market timing of the sale of IBM. I was selling more from the heart than from the head. I was selling IBM out of a sense of stubbornness and moral principle that happened to work out well. Over the long term, Harry was right that you should invest with your head and not your heart. It's best, however, when one can invest with both in alignment.

***

If a business does well, the stock eventually follows.
—Warren Buffett

Payback

After graduating from college in June of 1953, Harry entered the United States Marine Corps, along with a number of his friends from college. He entered the service because the Korean War was still being fought, and he simply believed that it was the right thing to do.

Harry went straight to Officer Candidate School in Quantico, Virginia, for training as a Marine Corps officer. It was grueling training, similar to what I experienced in Pensacola, Florida, when I signed up to enter the navy's flight program. The drill instructors were tough on the new recruits, and they put them through all kinds of physical and mental stress to make sure that the men they made officers could effectively lead US Marines into battle in Korea.

It was so intense that for the ninety days the training lasted, the recruits often viewed the drill instructors as the enemy against whom they somehow needed to survive. For the smallest of individual infractions, based on a myriad of seemingly ridiculous rules, the drill instructors would punish the entire group. Needless to say, Harry and his fellow officer candidates did not like the drill instructors.

Before the graduation day for his class, one of his drill instructors suggested that the drill instructors and the candidates play a friendly game of touch football. Harry and the other candidates agreed to the game. Little did the drill instructors know that there were at least a dozen division one varsity football players and several All-American football players in the group.

By the end of the game, Harry and his teammates had more than made up for the drill instructors' previous wrongdoings. The injury count was high, and many of the drill instructors wound up in the infirmary. The score and the injury list ended up in favor of the candidates.

In a sobering twist of fate, Harry was injured during this game. He wrenched his knee, aggravating an old college football injury. Fortunately, during the few weeks it took him to recuperate, the United States and the Korean governments signed a peace agreement. Harry was commissioned a second lieutenant in the Marine Corps infantry. If he had gone to Korea only a few weeks earlier, then the odds that he would have been killed were greater than 50 percent.

The drill instructors had underestimated their opponents. Whether it is a twist of the knee or a twist of fate, things often happen for a reason. Life is strange this way. If Harry had not played in that football game and injured his knee, then I might never have been born.

***

Before setting out on revenge, first dig two graves.
—Chinese proverb

Patriotism

Harry was a deeply patriotic man, yet he did not wear it on his sleeve. He loved his country and had served as a marine, but he did it with a quiet sense of purpose. "It seemed like the right thing to do at the time," is all he would tell me when I asked him about the Marine Corps. Whether it was love of country or love of family, Harry grew up as part of a generation that was not comfortable sharing emotions. We all knew that he loved us, but he certainly didn't say it. He was affectionate with Mom, and he would wrestle and roughhouse with his two boys, but saying the words "I love you," or "I love America," was just not his style.

Whenever Alex or I would do something good in school or in sports, Harry would pat us on the back or tussle our hair, but it was always Mom who would need to whisper to us at bedtime that "your father is so proud of you. He loves you so much." This translation from Mom was always nice, but I know we both missed hearing it from Harry.

On one rare occasion, when a confluence of events brought his love of family and of country together, Harry let his guard down. It was at a party that my parents threw in my honor upon my return home after the first Gulf War in 1991. As a navy carrier pilot, I had flown forty-five missions over Iraq and Kuwait. Many of my dearest friends and all my family were present. I will never forget when Harry asked the gathering for quiet so that he could say a few words.

I am sure that he said some nice things about me and about our country, but all that I remember him saying was, "I missed you, I love you, and I am so proud of you and of your service to our country." As he spoke these words, his voice cracked, and he started to cry. My eyes welled with tears as I walked up to him, and we hugged each other tightly.

While I knew that he had felt that way forever, both about me and about America, it felt so good for both of us to hear those words and share them. This is a life lesson I learned from Harry's general inability to do it. Say I love you, I miss you, and I am proud of you to your children often enough to let them know how you feel.

***

Actions speak louder than words, but words matter.

Fatherhood

It is impossible to appreciate the weighty responsibility of fatherhood until it actually happens. I cannot possibly write about how my father felt when I was born, but I can certainly describe how I felt when I became a father. There is no doubt that I am my father's son. So I believe that it is quite likely that my feelings on this topic of fatherhood, as well as the next few stories from my own experience, are well aligned with Harry's view of the world.

Nobody should ever underestimate the intensity of the pain experienced by the mother during childbirth. Especially with a first child, there is also a tremendous sense of uncertainty and a fear of the unknown. Even though billions of women have given birth for thousands of years, when it is the first time for the new mother; it is scary. The labor that Alice went through with our son Henry lasted over fifteen hours, and it was then followed by an emergency cesarean section operation. Alice was incredibly brave throughout the entire event, which was a nervous time for both of us.

Fortunately, our son Henry was healthy, and at the time of this writing, thirteen years later, he continues to be happy and healthy. The overwhelming feeling when I became a father was one of responsibility mixed with joy. Today our children are getting older, yet the three siblings are still dependent upon us. Parenting is an incredible responsibility because children represent the best and the worst of their parents. Every time I face a challenge as a father I ask, "What Harry would do?"

***

If the new American father feels bewildered and even defeated, let him take comfort from the fact that whatever he does in any fathering situation has a fifty percent chance of being right.
—Bill Cosby

Fate

Commander Ron Dargo. I will never forget his name. He was the commanding officer of VT-7 when I completed my advanced jet flight training. I remember the conversation as if it were yesterday. "Good afternoon, sir," I said in my best military tone. "Ensign Baldwin reporting for duty, sir. Standing by to receive my orders, sir."

Commander Dargo took off his reading glasses and stared directly at me. "I bet you want to fly Hornets."

"Yes, sir, that's what I have been working for over the past two years."

"Well, this piece of paper says that you are going to be flying EA-6B Prowlers from Whidbey Island."

"What?" I said. "What's an EA-6B Prowler? Please check the list again, sir. You must have been reading the wrong line."

"That's what the US Navy wants you to do. Go fly Prowlers, and be the best goddamn Prowler pilot that the navy has ever seen."

"Yes, sir!" I was standing rigid at attention, and I executed a small ninety-degree turn to exit his office. My feet knew the way down the stairs to the exit door of the hangar, but my mind was racing elsewhere. Every night for two years, I had gone to sleep looking above my bed at a picture of an FA-18 Hornet because I was convinced that I was going to fly that jet one day. This was my dream. I was absolutely crushed, heartbroken, dejected, and in shock.

I walked several hundred yards across the length of the parking lot and opened the door to my "Ricky Racer," a red 1989 Toyota Supra. I had bought the little red sports car because that was just what was done when you were a young navy carrier pilot. I reached for my keys to start the car and drive away, my head shaking side to side involuntarily. There was something wrong with this situation. My roommate must be playing a prank on me, and he had brought the CO of the squadron onboard. That must be it.

For years, I had dreamed about playing center field for the New York Mets. When that dream died a slow death while I was playing college baseball, I started to create a new dream, which was to fly F/A-18 Hornets for the navy. Now Commander Dargo was shattering that dream.

Not willing to believe Dargo's orders, I proceeded to walk several hundred yards back into the hangar and back up to his office. I knocked on the door and went in upon hearing the gruff "Enter." When he saw me again, CDR Dargo did not disguise his displeasure.

"Sir, I'm sorry to bother you, but I figure that my roommate must be playing a practical joke on me. Could you please double-check your list? I am quite sure that I should be flying Hornets."

"Baldwin, you are flying Prowlers, and if you don't get out of here now, you'll be flying a desk for the rest of your career!" shouted CDR Dargo.

Stunned and disappointed, I drove back to my apartment and called my parents. I had worked so hard to accomplish a specific goal, and while I had achieved a great deal in earning my navy wings, I somehow felt bitterly disappointed. I remember what Harry said to me during that phone call: "Remember what's important. You've earned your wings, which is a great accomplishment. You are serving your country, which is exactly what you want to be doing. You're very lucky. Sometimes things happen for a reason. Go fly the Prowler and see what happens."

Within a matter of days, I was deeply immersed in learning all there was to know about Prowlers and our demanding mission. Within nine months, I was forward deployed to the USS *Midway* shortly after Saddam Hussein invaded Kuwait. Before I knew it, I had flown forty-five combat missions over Iraq in a Prowler, while my friends who had been selected for Hornets on that fateful day were still in flight training because of delays in the training pipeline.

I never would have served in the first Gulf War, never would have met Alice, never would have written my first book, and never would have been able to conduct my current business without the many experiences that I had as a Prowler pilot. As Harry reminded me, "Sometimes things happen for a reason," and there are often unintended consequences from your choices in life.

***

We all have dreams. But in order to make dreams come into reality, it takes an awful lot of determination, dedication, self-discipline, and effort.
—Jesse Owens

I am explaining to Harry and Alex the finer points of tactical flying.

Persistence

His name was John, and he was my primary rival as early as fourth grade. We were both determined young athletes at a young age, and it seemed that every day we would look to find a new way to beat each other in some form of competition. Whether it was running, climbing, or throwing, in any form of athletic competition, one of us was number one, and the other was number two.

One day, John came to gym class with a big smile on his face. I knew that something was up. Sure enough, within minutes of the start of the gym class, John said, "Hey, guys, check out this trick." John proceeded to demonstrate a backbend. He stood up and put his hands straight up over his head. He then proceeded to bend slowly backward in a controlled way. Once he had tilted beyond the point of no return, he simply continued to bend until he dropped onto his hands. When he completed the maneuver, he still had his feet on the floor, as well as his hands.

Everyone simultaneously oohed and ahhed at John's new stunt.

"That doesn't look so hard," I said. "Here, watch me." I spoke with a level of confidence that belied my sense of trepidation. I stood tall, with my hands raised, and started to bend back toward the floor. Once my arms and weight took over and I started to fall over, I chickened out and bailed out on the backbend by falling on my ass.

"Nice backsit," said one of my classmates, chuckling. This was among many choice comments made to me as I sat on the floor, feeling completely defeated.

That night after dinner, I went to my room, took a pillow off my bed, and set it on the floor. I started trying backbends, hitting my head on the pillow with a thud. After hearing a number of thuds, Harry knocked on the door to my room.

"What the heck are you doing?" asked Harry. "You're going to hurt yourself."

"I just want to learn how to do a backbend," I said.

"What's a backbend?" asked Harry,

I tried another backbend and crashed again. "Well, I imagine that you will be the first kid in your class to be able to do a backbend," said Harry.

"That's the problem; there's already a kid who can do backbends."

"I see," said Harry. "Well, in that case, you better figure out the backbend tonight, and then come up with a new trick to keep him on his heels."

I did backbends and hit my head on the floor for several hours before I learned to control my body and arch my back gradually to enable me to do the backdrop. My parents listened to me hitting my head on the floor, and they realized that I was a determined and persistent young person. What they didn't know is that Harry's comments encouraged me to figure out how to stand back up after the backbend.

The next day, I went to gym class and demonstrated my new trick. I leaned back onto my hands, and then, after pausing briefly, I stood back up straight. John was flabbergasted because he could only do the backbend. He could not stand back up. His victory had been short-lived.

***

Nothing in the world can take the place of persistence. Talent will not; nothing is more common than unsuccessful men with talent. Genius will not; unrewarded genius is almost a proverb. Education will not; the world is full of educated derelicts. Persistence and determination alone are omnipotent.
—Calvin Coolidge

Leadership

Lead where there are clear problems and great opportunities, and
    manage the rest.

Encourage the heart; celebrate success along the way.

Avoid the counsel of your fears and naysayers.

Deliver extraordinary results.

Engage people to make commitments and listen for possibilities.

Respect the past, being realistic about the present and perpetually
    optimistic about the future.

Speak for what you believe, and do the right thing.

Have fun and create a fun environment.

Inspire a shared vision. Be passionate and demanding in seeing it
    through.

Pay attention to details.

My mnemonic of leadership principles was inspired by my father
Harry Baldwin and the Henry Crown Fellowship, and it includes some of
the ideas of General Colin Powell and professors Carol and Jack Weber.
I have collected, refined and aggregated these principles over the years,
and I believe they hold true.

Some of the best leadership development training that I have ever
received was during my years in the United States Navy. When I was
commissioned an officer in the U.S. Navy, Master Gunnery Sergeant D.
W. Bearup, the chief drill instructor at Aviation Officer Candidate School
in Pensacola, Florida, gave me a small card. On it was a note from the
Master Gunnery Sergeant:

You can divide naval officers into two classes: **Pretenders** and **Contenders.** The Pretenders are the ones who never sacrifice themselves. They will never understand the meaning of "total dedication"; therefore, they will never taste the glory. The Contenders are the ones who demand of themselves the absolute maximum limit and are willing to pay that price. They will be able to catch the glory. Life is that way. There are Pretenders, and there are Contenders. The question is … which one are you?

—Master Gunnery Sergeant D. W. Bearup, USMC
Chief Drill Instructor, Aviation Officer Candidate School

This card, given to me twenty years ago, still sits in a small plastic frame in my office at home. I believe it captures the essence of life's great question: how do you want to choose to lead your life? For it is a choice. Nothing is preordained. A person can choose. In life, there are leaders, and there are followers. There are Pretenders and Contenders.

I will never forget my drill instructor leaning forward so that the brim of his Smokey the Bear hat touched my forehead. I could smell the mix of coffee and cigars on his breath when he said to me, "There are Pretenders, and there are Contenders. The question is…. which one are you?"

***

Leadership is the art of getting someone else to do something you want done because he wants to do it.
—Dwight D. Eisenhower

Possibilities

One of the most powerful phrases that I know is "Up until now...." The words set the tone for change. Today, change is a part of life, and it will be more a part of our children's lives than for any generation before them. Things are changing at a dizzying pace, and what is true today will not necessarily be true tomorrow. For this reason, it is so important for people to ground themselves in fundamental truths and values that will help them adapt and make choices when things are changing around them.

I encourage my children to engage in what one might call "possibility thinking." I first learned this term from professors Jack and Carol Weber at the Darden School of Management at the University of Virginia. The concept is simple and powerful. Instead of thinking about what is probable or appropriate, it is important to think about what is possible. Harry did not think this way. Harry was more of a skeptic, and it is perhaps the biggest negative lesson that I learned from him, meaning that I did not want to think like a skeptic. At the core of possibility thinking is an optimism that just about anything is possible.

When faced with a daunting challenge, possibility thinking forces you to ask the question, "How can we make this happen?" This question is so much more exciting than the alternative, which is to focus your energy on all the myriad of obstacles in the way of making it happen. Of course, it is critical to consider the obstacles and treat them realistically, but no great leader was ever a pessimist.

***

We all have possibilities we don't know about. We can do things we don't even dream we can do.
—Dale Carnegie

Carpe Diem

The Latin expression "carpe diem" translates in English as "seize the day." Even though I am more of an optimist than Harry was, we shared a love for this phrase, and for a movie called *Breaker Morant*, which was the name of the captain leading a small company of British soldiers during the Boer War in South Africa.

The Boer War was an unpopular war both on the British home front and in South Africa. Executing orders, Captain Morant led his troops on a raid of a small band of Boer guerrillas and killed most of them. Unfortunately for Morant and his men, who thought they were following orders, the British politicians were trying to resolve the conflict and end the war. Morant and his men were imprisoned and charged with murder in order to appease the Boer politicians and gain a peace agreement.

A young military lawyer defended Morant and his men valiantly, but at the end of the day, Morant and his men were sentenced to death by firing squad as a sacrifice to the peace negotiations.

Morant's last words, as he stood before the firing squad, were simple and straightforward: "Live each day as if it were your last, for someday you are sure to be right." He then paused and yelled, "Shoot straight, you bastards!"

"Those poor guys were just executing their orders," lamented Harry.

"The government sure turned on them, didn't they?" I added.

"It certainly proves Murphy's Law," said Harry with a smile. "We all need to live each day as if it were our last." At the time, Harry had no way of knowing that Breaker Morant's fate would happen sooner in his own life than he or anyone else expected.

***

Older men declare war. But it is the youth that must fight and die.
—Herbert Hoover

Courage

While I never saw Harry in a life-threatening situation—where bullets were flying, or where he was in grave imminent personal danger, as in the story of Breaker Morant—I know that he was a courageous man, for he faced a terrible disease and stared certain death in the eye over an extended period of nine months. He demonstrated phenomenal courage every day. This was never more true than on the day that he died.

In January of 1997, Harry told me that he had a horrible disease called ALS, or Lou Gehrig's disease. Nine months later, he died in a hospital bed, a few minutes before I arrived to join my mom at the hospital. The disease mysteriously attacks the muscles and leaves the body a shell of its former self. The muscles gradually deteriorate as the disease robs them of their strength. For an athletic, vibrant man, "the strongest man I have ever known," ALS was a cruel disease. It weakened his body, but his spirit remained strong.

As we grew up, Alex and I would wrestle on the floor with him in a playful way, like puppies with a dog. After putting up with us for a while, he'd finally decide that enough was enough, and we would feel iron grips on our thighs, which he called the "horse bite." It felt like a vise tightening on my leg. These powerful fingers deteriorated over the year that he suffered from ALS, and on the morning that he died, he was unable to button his shirt. His hands trembled, and he needed to concentrate just to do basic tasks. He fought the disease in his own courageous way. He told it to go to hell.

On that last morning, when he went with Mom to the hospital, Harry pulled himself out of his motorized chair and shaved his face in the bathroom, as he had done every day for over fifty years. It was his way of saying to the disease, "You have not beaten me, and I refuse to bow down to you. I will continue to do just what I have done as if I were still healthy." It was a small victory, but sometimes courage lies in the small things.

Life knocks each of us down sometimes. Whether it's failing a test, losing a game, losing a job, or being hurt by a loved one, the true test of character is how a person reacts when knocked down. What matters is to keep getting up, to keep fighting. This is everyday courage. Perhaps not the stuff of movies, but remember that movies are not real. The people with real courage are overcoming obstacles every day so that they can pay the rent, put food on the table, and buy clothes for their children. Everyday courage enables people to keep getting up for another day of living.

When I got to the hospital, Mom was there with him. Through her tears, she simply said, "He's gone ... he's gone." He lay there with his mouth agape in bed. He no longer looked like Harry. Mom was right; he was gone. His fighting spirit had already left his body.

Whatever fears Harry had, he overcame them every day because he knew that our family depended on him. Every day, he would get up and go to the office to make an honest living so that his children could get an education and our family could have a safe home. He was the most courageous man I have ever known.

***

Courage is not the absence of fear, but the capacity for action despite our fears.
—John McCain

Never, never, never give up.
—Winston Churchill

It is not the critic who counts: not the man who points out how the strong man stumbles or where the doer of deeds could have done better. The credit belongs to the man who is actually in the arena, whose face is marred by dust and sweat and blood, who strives valiantly, who errs and comes up short again and again, because there is no effort without error or shortcoming, but who knows the great enthusiasms, the great devotions, who spends himself for a worthy cause; who, at the best, knows, in the end, the triumph of high achievement, and who, at the worst, if he fails, at least he fails while daring greatly, so that his place shall never be with those cold and timid souls who know neither victory nor defeat.

"Citizenship in a Republic"
Speech at the Sorbonne, Paris
April 23, 1910
—Theodore Roosevelt

Character

Harry understood that character is a trait that is tested every day and that a person's character is a work in progress every day of his or her life. When Harry was diagnosed with Lou Gehrig's disease, he viewed the disease as is his opportunity to demonstrate courage and make it clear to all watching that in his final days, he remained a man of character to the end.

The doctors believe that Harry may well have had early onset of the disease two years prior to the diagnosis, but his tough and stoic nature made him think, "I'm just getting old." As the disease progressed, Harry was unable to do many of the basic things in life. I thought of Harry as a prisoner of war in his own body. American prisoners of war are trained to resist their captors with small acts of defiance each day. For example, prisoners of war during Vietnam often stood at attention in the prison camps with their hands at their sides and their middle fingers extended in defiance of their captors. The mission of an American prisoner of war is to resist and to escape. It seemed that Harry did things to avoid giving in to the disease. Harry showed small acts of defiance to his disease up until the very end.

His defiant attitude started with his delay in getting diagnosed. One could simply view it as denial, but he refused to believe that he could be succumbing to such a horrible fate. To thumb his nose at the disease, Harry would laugh whenever possible, but as the disease progressed, the laugh changed. It was no longer the trademark laugh that attracted people from the other side of the room; it became a mere shadow of what it had once been. He would hold his two-year-old grandson, my son Henry, in his weakening arms, and he would race along in his motorized

119

chair. Whether it was brushing his teeth or shaving, Harry did everything he could to continue a normal life and to defy his captor.

Harry made the most of his opportunity in this world. He lived a full life, even if it was shorter than any of us would have liked. Each day, he took advantage of the opportunity to live a life of integrity, respect, courage, and commitment. In so doing, he was a man of character.

***

There is no heavier burden than a great opportunity.
—Thomas Jefferson

Harry with me and his first grandchild, Henry.

Henry deForest Baldwin
"Harry"
1931–1997

1931   Born in New York City to Harriett Rantoul Baldwin and Sherman Baldwin, October 22

1934   Sister, Lois, born April 8

1948   Graduated Pomfret School, June

1949   Attended Edinburgh Academy, Scotland

1953   Graduated Yale University, Pierson College, June

1953   Enlisted in United States Marine Corps to serve in the Korean War

1959   Graduated from University of Michigan Law School and joined Lord, Day & Lord

1962   Married Martha Mosby Denniston in Philadelphia, May 5

1964   Sherman Baldwin born, June 18

1967   Elected partner of law firm Lord, Day & Lord

1968   Alexander Denniston Baldwin born, January 29

1969   Founding director of the Roxbury Land Trust

1984   Elected managing partner of Lord, Day & Lord

1990   Lord, Day & Lord, Barrett Smith dissolved

1991   Joins Morgan, Lewis & Bockius as a partner

1997   Diagnosed with ALS in January. Dies in September.

Harry's Memorial Service

9/6/97

My dad loved to laugh, and his laugh was deep, heartfelt, and infectious. Countless family meals were dominated by long, loud fits of laughter as we shared stories and jokes with each other. On one such occasion, in a dimly lit and normally quiet French restaurant here in New York, we were all laughing hysterically. When the main course arrived, our boisterous behavior was interrupted by a stranger who walked out of the shadows from the other side of the restaurant. He extended his hand to my dad, saying, "You must be Harry Baldwin, Yale class of nineteen fifty-three. I'd recognize that laugh anywhere." He had not seen my dad in years, but he knew there was only one man who could laugh like Dad. And upon reflection, I think it is a great thing to be known for your laugh.

I am not sure if my dad inherited his laugh from his father; but I do know that his father, Sherman Baldwin, who is my namesake, was universally respected. As I was growing up, friends and family members would always tell me stories of my grandfather and say to me, "Sherman, your grandfather was such a special man." Sadly, I was only five years old when he died.

When I was old enough to read, I found a framed clipping about my grandfather from the *New York Times* hanging in my parents' bedroom. The clipping was a reprint of the eulogy that had been delivered at his memorial service in 1969, here at the Brick Church. I feel strongly that some of those words are just as fitting for my dad today as they were fitting for his father twenty-eight years ago. So as I try to capture what my dad meant to all of us, I would like to share with you the last two sentences of my grandfather's eulogy: "And lastly his love for his family—a love complete and true, and nearest of all to the center of his being. All in all, his qualities of mind and spirit came as near perfection as a man can come."

My son Henry deForest Baldwin is not even three years old today, and I am so deeply saddened that it will be difficult for him to remember my dad, his namesake. So, as the son of one Henry deForest Baldwin, and the father of the next generation's Henry deForest Baldwin, I ask all of you here today, and in the coming years, to share your memories of my dad with my son. In this way, we will all be able to keep his memory alive in our hearts and hear his laughter ringing in our ears.

Bibliography

1. Brown, H. Jackson Jr. *A Father's Book of Wisdom*. Nashville. Rutledge Hill Press, Inc., 1988.

2. Lewis, Michael. *Coach*. New York. W. W. Norton & Company, Inc., 2005.

3. McCain, John, and Marshall Salter. *Why Courage Matters*. New York. Random House, 2004.

4. Stoddard, Alexandra. *Things I Want My Daughters to Know*. New York. Harper Collins, 2004.

5. Trillin, Calvin. *About Alice*. New York. Random House, 2006.

Notes

The quotes at the end of each chapter are attributed to their speaker or author as appropriate. The attributed quotes were researched from two public domain Web sites: BrainyQuote.com and QuoteDB.com. The simple sentences at the end of a chapter that are not cited represent my personal perspective on the preceding chapter.

978-0-595-45291-0
0-595-45291-4

Printed in the United Kingdom
by Lightning Source UK Ltd.
R851500001BA/R8515PG130101UKX2BA/1-18/P